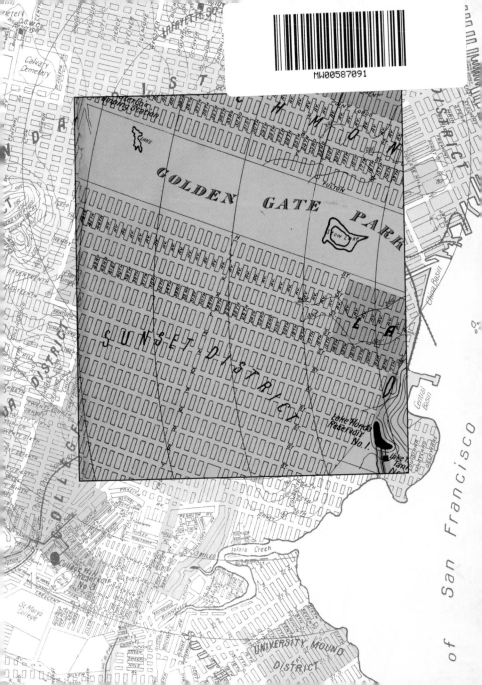

SAN FRANCISCO
COCKTAILS

AN ELEGANT COLLECTION
OF OVER 100 RECIPES
INSPIRED BY THE CITY BY THE BAY

TREVOR FELCH

CIDER MILL
PRESS

BOOK
PUBLISHERS
KENNEBUNKPORT, MAINE

SAN FRANCISCO COCKTAILS

ISBN-13: 978-1-64643-019-2
ISBN-10: 1-64643-019-0

This book may be ordered by mail from the publisher. Please include $5.99 for postage and handling. Please support your local bookseller first!

Books published by Cider Mill Press Book Publishers are available at special discounts for bulk purchases in the United States by corporations, institutions, and other organizations. For more information, please contact the publisher.

Cider Mill Press Book Publishers
"Where good books are ready for press"
PO Box 454
12 Spring Street
Kennebunkport, Maine 04046
Visit us online!
cidermillpress.com

Typography: Farmhand Sans, Avenir, Copperplate, Sackers, Warnock

Photography Credits on page 387

Printed in China

2 3 4 5 6 7 8 9 0

CONTENTS

INTRODUCTION

At around 49 square miles and surrounded by three sides of water preventing any sprawling growth, San Francisco isn't ever going to be confused with the mega metropolises of the world. Then, combine the city's strict building codes with its physical boundaries and there is no way that San Francisco can grow much more. It will always be a small big city; not a big city. After all, San Francisco isn't even the most populated Bay Area city (that would be San Jose).

On the other hand, San Francisco is a city unlike any other in non-quantifiable ways. It's a city of poetry, where tourists leave their hearts (and heavy credit card bills) and residents move away, only to return months later because the gravitational pull is too strong to resist (usually thanks to the beautiful weather).

San Francisco is a town with sweeping beauty, where ocean waves crash to the west, cable cars roar up Russian Hill, buffalo roam in Golden Gate Park (it's true), and the stunning Bay Bridge and Golden Gate Bridge make even the most curmudgeonly longtime local stop to admire them.

San Francisco is a town of gold and sea lions; of stagecoaches and amazing arts; of computers and Beat Generation writers; of Barbary Coast pirates and tech hackers.

But, let's not get too far ahead of ourselves about what San Francisco really is, because what truly makes San Francisco San Francisco is how it lets everyone and everything express their independence.

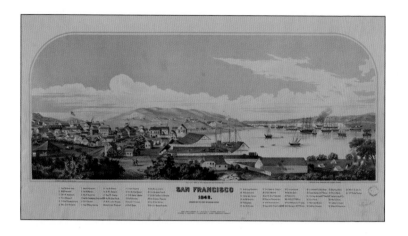

This is where everyone can put a flower in their hair and find somebody to love, as Scott McKenzie and Grace Slick sang.

There are some things, however, that do tie together this fun and funky city. Outside of rooting for the home teams (baseball's Giants, basketball's Warriors, football's 49ers), eating and drinking are always the topic of the day in San Francisco. The local, organic, seasonal cooking movement, which can now be found in every corner of the globe, is generally acknowledged to have started just across the Bay at Alice Waters's historic Chez Panisse in Berkeley. Northern California's temperate climate (virtually no snowfall) and diverse geography (pretty much everything except deserts and frozen tundra) make it ideal for just about every ingredient that can go on a menu, from local anchovies and oysters to fresh buffalo milk mozzarella and the juiciest heirloom tomatoes imaginable. That same sparkling climate and varied geography equation also makes the region home to some of the world's most acclaimed wine regions (heard of the Napa Valley?). Even some of the world's most iconic craft breweries also reside in San Francisco and its neighboring cities. After all, as was pointed out to me by Duggan McDonnell, one of San Francisco's leading modern cocktail bartenders and historians (see page 23), San Francisco's main water source is Hetch Hetchy Reservoir in Yosemite National Park, which is often considered some of the best tasting water in the world. So, of course, anything using water, like beer, coffee, or ice, is great here!

If there is one time of day, though, for eating or drinking that connects our San Francisco in the third decade of the 21st century with the San Francisco of preceding centuries, it would be cocktail hour. When the Ferry Building clock rings five times at 5:00 pm, it's basically the official signal that it's time for a cocktail, as it might have felt like in that same neighborhood when bartending legend Jerry Thomas served drinks 170 or so years ago (there would have been no Ferry Building in the 1850, however, because that wasn't built until 1898).

The world doesn't look at San Francisco as an "old" city like a Philadelphia or New York, but it was the year 1776 when Spanish missionaries founded Mission Dolores in San Francisco, the mission today that is the namesake for the neighborhood that I'd argue is the single greatest cocktail neighborhood in the country (see page 68). I'm pretty

sure there was something else happening that same year 3,000 miles to the east in Philadelphia.

Just a few decades later in the mid-1800s, San Francisco (previously called "Yerba Buena") truly became an internationally known boomtown and critical port thanks to the Gold Rush near the Sierra Nevada Mountains, east of the city. San Francisco was full of saloons, bars, and brothels, especially in the nightlife area of the "Barbary Coast," which is now the area around North Beach and Jackson Square, but back then was the waterfront, until landfill building pushed the Bay further and further toward the east and north. "When San Francisco was finding its footing as a city, cocktails and drinking were very important," explains Rich Table's Larry Piakowsky, one of the leading cocktail bartenders today, and a tremendous cocktail industry scholar. It was in this growth period of the mid to late 1800s when Jerry Thomas, author of the seminal *The Bartender's Guide: A Complete Cyclopedia of Plain and Fancy Drinks*, tended bar at San Francisco's Occidental Hotel and might have created the martini and/or the Martinez cocktail. Maybe he did? Maybe he didn't? Nobody will ever truly know, but there's no doubt how important he was as a bartender at the time.

Duncan Nichols invented the Pisco Punch in this same era, at another bar just a few steps away from the Occidental Hotel. Pisco was a critical part of San Francisco's trade economy and the libations that fueled it. Remember, there were no trains from the east coast back then (the Transcontinental Railroad's golden spike was hammered in 1869) and there was no Panama Canal. Goods coming from the east had to be shipped under South America's Cape Horn, usually stopping in Peru. Then goods and pisco would continue on ships to San Francisco's pisco-filled port. Peru's history with San Francisco is extensive—as leading Bay Area cocktail authority Virginia Miller mentioned to me, even Domingo Ghirardelli's (yes, the creator of Ghirardelli

G, SAN FRANCISCO, CAL.

Chocolate) first confectionary store opened in Lima, Peru, when he lived there between his childhood in Italy and moving to San Francisco during the Gold Rush.

If San Francisco in the 19th century was still in its Wild West adolescence, the 20th century was an adult period punctuated by landmark events or movements in every decade. There was the Great San Francisco 1906 Earthquake and subsequent fire that destroyed much of the city, followed by Prohibition and the Great Depression. Despite those being generally down years from a societal and economic perspective, they were actually still important cocktail times, with bar-

tender "Cocktail" William Boothby plying his trade in the early 1900s. In the Prohibition years, San Francisco, being its rebellious self, actually ignored the federal mandates for the most part. Bars like the historic Tosca Café in North Beach bent the rules or just skipped the rules. "Tosca kept themselves alive through Prohibition with those house Cappuccinos," says Miller, referring to the boozy, coffee-free cocktails created during Prohibition that remain a staple at Tosca today, albeit having had its recipe changed over the years (see page 49).

SAN FRANCISCO AND THE BAY AREA

Why San Francisco and the whole Bay Area in this book, but only San Francisco for the name? Well, first of all, we're not the only "Bay Area," as our friends in Tampa/St. Petersburg like to remind us. We need to always include "San Francisco" for reference when initially referring to this Bay Area. Second, San Francisco is certainly the main stage for the Bay Area—the center of business, tourism, and media. It's where the heavy majority of the action is when it comes to cocktails, both in terms of the number of bars and magnitude of importance of those bars in the conversation of cocktail history. So, we singled out San Francisco because it's the iconic, understandable main city of cocktails in Northern California. San Francisco is almost like a spirit. The cocktails of the city are the spiritual core of this book, complemented by all of the neighboring regions.

However, it is crucial to highlight the importance that the entire Bay Area has had on both San Francisco cocktails and cocktails around the world. By nature of the urban-suburban commute relationship, suburbs around the world are closely connected with their major cities. I'm not saying that Bay Area suburbs are any closer to San Francisco than in other major metro areas. What I am saying is how the cocktail scene is so strong in these suburbs and other cities. To not discuss Sebastopol, Oakland, and Los Gatos cocktails with San Francisco's cocktails is to miss a critical part of the whole San Francisco cocktails story. Yes, some of our greatest bars in the Bay Area are not in San Francisco. That is how spoiled we are here. And we certainly appreciate that wealth of options in all directions of San Francisco. We're all connected by bridges, railway tracks, ferries, and BART rails.

The city played a key strategic role in World War II, being home to many forts, military bases, and shipbuilding facilities (the Kaiser Shipyards in Richmond, a waterfront city in the East Bay, built 747 ships according to the National Park Service, which is why it is now home to the Rosie the Riveter/World War II Home Front National Historical Park). During these war years, "Trader Vic" Victor Bergeron invented the Mai Tai in 1944 and Nob Hill's Tonga Room opened a year later, both clearly showing that San Franciscans were in need of escape to a tropical wonderland, and so the tiki movement blossomed into full form from the shores of the chilly San Francisco Bay—a world away from the South Pacific.

The 1950s brought the Irish coffee to the Buena Vista from Ireland and the Giants to the city from New York, two pillars of San Francisco culture today. San Francisco's culture of self-expression and self-independence then proved itself more than ever in the ensuing two decades. "Being a place of freedom, people could always come here and be themselves, whether it was the 60s with the flower children, or the 70s and the Sexual Revolution," says Piakowsky. "San Francisco was always that place." The 60s and 70s saw Napa Valley wine soar to worldwide prominence and in 1976, a computer company named Apple started in the South Bay city of Cupertino. That period also brought tremendous tragedy to the city when gay rights leader and city supervisor Harvey Milk was assassinated along with Mayor George Moscone. Those events, combined with the AIDS crisis in the early 1980s and the powerful Loma Prieta earthquake of 1989, made for a challenging stretch of San Francisco history.

Amidst all of that tumult, San Francisco's cocktail scene was not of particular note, outside of Julio Bermejo deciding to skip orange liqueurs and forgettable premade lime juice for fresh lime juice and agave nectar in the margaritas at his Outer Richmond neighborhood establishment, Tommy's. Beyond Tommy's Margarita bright spot, trendy drinks were generally sweet or bland, often ending with "-tini" and altogether forgettable. But luckily, this was when Bay Area chefs were having their moment of tying together the best of Asian and European cooking techniques with California's bountiful produce. Bartenders in the late 90s at places like Absinthe Brasserie & Bar, Foreign Cinema, and 15 Romolo realized, wait, with all of these great ingredients why can't we make cocktails as noteworthy as the food? As Miller calls it, "the renaissance" for cocktails was underway.

Quality-focused cocktail programs steadily grew in the early 2000s. Bourbon & Branch, Rye, and The Alembic, three bars that continue to lead the top tier of San Francisco cocktail establishments, all opened in 2006. And on it goes even to this day. For the first two decades of this century, San Francisco has seen establishment after establishment open that puts the same focus on cocktails—either classic and meticulous, or creative and compelling; always with the best of homemade ingredients and spirits—that our world-renowned restaurants do for dishes from the kitchen. Many of our bars develop the trends that you'll see at your neighborhood bars in the ensuing years all around the world. Bars like Trick Dog and Smuggler's Cove seem to win awards as if they're Meryl Streep and Tom Hanks. And this influence has spread out all around the Bay Area. From Napa Valley to San Jose to Berkeley to Healdsburg, there are wonderful cocktails to be found all over the region.

Indeed, this is how your heart gets left in San Francisco. It's a small city with the biggest and best parts of the major world players, stirred (or shaken) with some quirkiness, stunning beauty, and exceptional creativity.

COVID-19 IN SAN FRANCISCO

As an author, it's very rare to be covering a subject for a book when arguably the most critical crisis of the book subject's history is unfolding unpredictably live, right before you. When I started on this assignment in 2019, there is no way that I could have expected that the COVID-19 pandemic would exist and what it would do to San Francisco—and the world—months later as my book deadline grew nearer. What would Hemingway have done, staring down the pressure of a book deadline, with no bar to visit? As I sit here in San Francisco on the fourteenth day of a shelter-in-place order, I can't go to a bar right now even if I wanted to. They are all closed in San Francisco. And the whole Bay Area. And the entire state of California. And many other states around the country. As far as I can find in my research, the only possible forced bar closure in recent times was for World War II. In a 2019 San Francisco Chronicle article looking back at archive coverage of V-E Day in 1945, writer Peter Hartlaub says, "Stores and churches were open on V-E Day, but bars were still closed."

Right now, bars and restaurants are frantically trying to figure out how to make money and keep employees paid without actually being open. In high-rent San Francisco, that is hardly a trivial thing to do. As I write this, one of our contributors, Locanda, announced their closure. Some other contributing bartenders have informed me that they were laid off.

Nobody knows when restaurants and bars will open again. It's open-ended at this point. Many restaurants have pivoted to offering takeout and delivery options. The state of California even allowed bars to sell to-go cocktails (as long as you open them at home) which has led bartenders to spend hours figuring out how to make the delicate art of cocktail making into one adapted for a portable drink. Some examples of drinks that I could enjoy at my home right now:

Mai o Mai, True Laurel
Chartreuse Slushy, The Morris
Margarita, Tommy's
Vampiro, Elda
Five Spot, Maven
Irish coffee, The Buena Vista

Will to-go cocktails become the next trend for cocktails once normal life returns? We've already seen cocktails on tap (Kevin Diedrich's Negroni on tap at Jasper's Corner Tap & Kitchen jump-started that trend in the city in 2011). In places like the Virgin Islands and New Orleans, people are always enjoying cocktails to-go. Maybe we're going in that social distancing direction?

But, San Francisco doesn't have a tropical beach or a Bourbon Street. We're a city built of hills and bars. A huge part of a cocktail's joy is the experience of being at a bar, watching the bartender make the drink, and chatting with friends and strangers.

Hopefully the San Francisco food and drink scene will weather this storm, yet another challenge of many that it has seen over the decades. It is a city that bounced back many times from all kinds of challenges before, rising as if the cable cars tug the city uphill away from the day's trouble. Let's raise a glass to the bars, the bartenders, and the decades of patrons that continue to add to the mystique and joy that is enjoying a cocktail in San Francisco. Cheers!

—March 30, 2020

BAY AREA COCKTAIL HOME BAR

Is your apartment the next Trick Dog or True Laurel? Here's a good place to start for cocktail basics combined with the best of the Bay Area. Feel free to go all out with a bar cart, decanters filled with Cognac, modernist sous-vide and carbonation things, and fresh fruits and herbs from your garden as decorations on your kitchen counter. However, let's be real, those are definitely not essentials for a Tuesday night Negroni or impressing guests at a party.

GLASSWARE

Collins glass

Coupe

Irish coffee mug

Cocktail glass

Rocks glass and larger double-rocks glass

Some sort of tiki mug

TOOLS

Bar spoon

Basic measuring tool

Cocktail picks

Hamilton Beach blender

Ice cube trays for large rocks and spheres

Mixing glass

Muddler

Paring knife

Peeler

Punch bowl

Shaker

Stainless-steel jigger

Strainers (conical, hawthorne, julep)

SPIRITS

209 gin (any kind)

Anchor Junipero Gin

Añejo tequila

The Botanist Gin

Bourbon

Bulleit Rye

Cachaça

Calvados

Clear Creek Douglas Fir
  Eau de Vie
Charbay Raspberry Vodka
Charbay Whiskey (any of
  the many expressions)
Cognac
Del Maguey Mezcal
Gaijer Aquavit
Hangar One Vodka
Hanson's of Sonoma
  Vodka
Japanese whisky
Loch & Union American
  Dry Gin
Reposado Tequila
Rhum agricole
Rum (dark)
Rum (a regular style)
Saint Benevolence Clairin
St. George Gin (any)
St. George Absinthe
St. George Green Chile
  Vodka
Scotch
Spirit Works Sloe Gin
Tullamore D.E.W. Irish
  Whiskey
Workhorse Rye
Liqueurs/Amaros
Campari

Green and yellow
  Chartreuse
Cointreau
Cynar
Disaronno Amaretto
Dolin Dry Vermouth
Dolin Sweet Vermouth
Fernet Branca
Fernet Leopold
Hello Cello! Limoncello di
  Sonoma
Lo-Fi Aperitifs
Luxardo Maraschino
Ramazotti
St. Germain Elderflower
  Liqueur
St. George NOLA Coffee
Velvet falernum
Bitters, Syrups, and Tonic
Angostura
BitterGirl Bitters
Bittermens Bitters
Bitter Truth
Ginger beer
Jack Rudy Elderflower
  Tonic
Perfect Purée
  concentrates
Peychaud's
Small Hand Foods
Tonic water

FERNET BRANCA

Of all the puzzling questions in the San Francisco bar world, the most curious one is: "Why is Fernet Branca so popular here?" It still startles me when I travel around the world and bartenders ask if I'd like a shot of Fernet Branca because, well, that's what we supposedly love to do in San Francisco. In reality, it's something that has been slightly overblown into a myth. I have seen numbers wildly vary that San Francisco consumes between 25% and 70% of the United States' imported Fernet Branca, the mint-forward, dense, very assertive Italian amaro/digestivo. I can almost guarantee that 70% is way too high a figure because, thanks to its original popularity in San Francisco in the 2000s and first half of the 2010s, many other major American cities have now discovered Fernet Branca's mystique. Fernet Branca's claim to fame in San Francisco is because bartenders sometimes would have a shot of it when closing their shift or as a celebratory gesture with a regular guest. From my non-scientific observations, it seems like mezcal and other types of amaro are now sharing that role with Fernet Branca. That being said, Fernet Branca has also crept into the world of cocktails, as bartenders are now creating clever cocktails using its unique flavor profile.

So, back to the *why* it is (or was) so popular here? I can give three reasons: 1) There has been a lot of marketing of Fernet Branca within the San Francisco bars and San Francisco food and drink media industry, 2) San Francisco was an early advocate for bitter, tart flavors in drinks, 3) San Francisco and Italy have a deep food and drink connection that covers everything from wine and liqueurs to pizza and seasonal produce.

THE DEFINITIVE SAN FRANCISCO SOUNDTRACK AND MOVIE ROSTER

"I Left My Heart in San Francisco"—Tony Bennett

"Sittin' on the Dock of the Bay"—Otis Redding

"Don't Stop Believin'!"—Journey

"If You're Going to San Francisco"—Scott McKenzie

"Red Red Wine" —UB40

"Tell Me When to Go"—E-40

"Somebody to Love"—Jefferson Airplane

"Oye Como Va"—Carlos Santana

Mrs. Doubtfire

The Maltese Falcon

Bullitt

Dirty Harry

Vertigo

Blue Jasmine

DUGGAN MCDONNELL

BARTENDER AND AUTHOR

For San Francisco cocktail history with a couple dashes of whimsy, Duggan McDonnell's *Drinking the Devil's Acre* is absolutely mandatory reading. McDonnell is one of our city's most eloquent cocktail voices and also one of our top cocktail talents. If you asked around about the most important now closed cocktail bar from this century, the answer would be McDonnell's Cantina, near Union Square (it then became Pacific Cocktail Haven, and, sadly, had a fire in 2021; rebuilding is in the works). McDonnell and I corresponded about past and current San Francisco cocktail history in the Devil's Acre and well beyond.

FIRST OFF, LET'S START IN THE PAST. CAN YOU TELL US A BIT ABOUT HOW YOU GOT INTERESTED IN THE WHOLE HIGH-QUALITY COCKTAILS PROFESSION WHEN IT WAS STILL A RELATIVELY NEW IDEA?

I wrote my first cocktail menu in 2003 while working as the general manager for the Redwood Room, in the Clift Hotel. It wasn't earth-shattering stuff, but the fruit and herb ingredients were fresh, the spirits lux, and technique crisp. I'm a Bay Area native, and I'd only worked in fine dining restaurants with a commitment to excellent cuisine and drinks—it was an organic experience, and I was simply a product of my culture. Folks may not know that there wasn't a formed community at the time, as the USBG had yet to be formally realized in the city. As such, I didn't have a single experience of a restaurant or bartender doing this work. I had no expectations, only my imagination and what I believed was possible! To me, the connection was obvious: if people are eating well, shopping for fresh food, the cocktails should match.

WHO WERE SOME OF THE MAJOR PLAYERS IN LAYING THE GROUNDWORK FOR THE CRAFT COCKTAIL MOVEMENT IN SAN FRANCISCO AND WHAT INFLUENCE DID THEY HAVE ON YOU?

In *Drinking the Devil's Acre*, I wrote about working side-by-side with Marco Dionysos in Harry Denton's Starlight Room in 2003 before I joined the Redwood Room. The menu then was largely written by Tony Abou-Ganim from several years prior with a few classic cocktails added by Marco. At the time, I didn't much care for classic cocktail revival, as my intellect is bent on creating, not mimicking—no offense to the masters of this craft. What I did most appreciate about Marco was his utter physicality. In that era, he operated in full-on Beast Mode while I was a fledgling Boy Scout. The dude shook, stirred, did everything fast!

We've been using this expression of "craft cocktails" extensively and exclusively, but it's a misnomer. A craft is a profession, fixing shoes, making furniture. And in San Francisco a craft approach did emerge with Marco back at Absinthe in 1998, and was largely established by Bourbon & Branch in 2006. But, this trend is divergent from San Francisco's history and I certainly wasn't a part of that movement—I led the way in cocktail creation, in applying improvisation to recipes, wild combinations such as mezcal, salted caramel, and horseradish over a single cube, back in 2004, and mentored teams of bartenders to do the same. This created today's culture of Dealer's Choice and Barkeep's Whimsy—the utter joy of sitting down before a confident, culinary barkeep and letting her shake or stir up a prescription without being exactly prescriptive!

In 2004, a man sat down on a barstool before me at Frisson where I was managing its bar and cocktail program (dubbed a "Leader of the American Cocktail Revolution" in *Food + Wine*). He ordered a drink and after introducing himself, asked for my advice on how to run his cocktail program at a new restaurant in Healdsburg. I told him he had it all in his own backyard: the fresh herbs, the produce so vibrant in every season. He just needed to showcase the bounty of the land in every glass. In a matter of months that man emerged as the cocktail genius he is today: Scott Beattie (see page 313).

WHAT LED YOU TO OPEN CANTINA? ANY FAVORITE TAKE-AWAYS OR STORIES FROM CANTINA'S GREAT RUN? AND, WHAT DO YOU FEEL HAS CHANGED ABOUT THE LOCAL COCKTAIL CROWD AND THEIR TASTES SINCE CANTINA'S CLOSING?

Many bartenders are inherently entrepreneurial. We yearn to have a place of our own. It's in our DNA. At the time, I was 32 years young and drafted a business plan and had the good fortune to open Cantina the following year in 2007. But, let's remember, running a business is different than running a beverage program and its creativity. Only the best can do both and still, there's a half-life for establishments in our industry. Let's hope the titans of today—Trick Dog, Pacific Cocktail Haven, Comstock Saloon—will be open for years to come.

Where Cantina succeeded is that it integrated an ecosystem of ideas; it didn't stay in a single lane as just a Latin spirits bar, or a team exhibiting exquisite cocktail technique, or as a hotspot featuring the best deejay's in the city spinning hip-hop while Scotch was shaken and mezcal stirred—it was all of those things while being incredibly welcoming to the hospitality community. During that first summer of 2007, my late friend Dahi Donnelly (who'd founded Bourbon + Branch with Brian Sheehy and Doug Dalton) was enjoying a cocktail inside Cantina and said to me: "My next bar is going to be like Cantina. Fun! I want people to enjoy their drink and have a fucking fun time!" And then, that talented group opened Rickhouse, and the rest is history.

More importantly, I like to remember that Cantina was a chapel of love. The drinks enchanted, the room was warm, and the lights low. Dozens of couples met and fell in love in that room. To this day, so many people tell of finding romance in that bar!

WHAT LED YOU TO THE WORLD OF PISCO AND FOUNDING YOUR OWN PISCO BRAND, CAMPO DE ENCANTO?

As I was preparing to open Cantina in 2007, I studied San Francisco's cocktail history, its great bartenders, and the historical tastes of our community. Pisco kept coming up, but it was forgotten. And in 2007, the information on the then-nascent internet was abysmal. The only thing in English was on Wikipedia, and I knew it was full of errors. On a whim, I thought I'd place a Pisco Punch on Cantina's first cocktail menu, proclaim I was returning to San Francisco its signature drink, and see what happened. The media picked this up and within the first week, in came master distiller Carlos Romero, with whom I later co-founded Campo de Encanto.

CAN YOU TELL US A BIT ABOUT PISCO'S RICH HISTORY WITH SAN FRANCISCO? OF COURSE, MANY LOCALS AND VISITORS KNOW THAT THE PISCO PUNCH WAS INVENTED HERE. BUT VERY FEW KNOW WHY THERE IS SUCH A LONGSTANDING RELA-TIONSHIP BETWEEN THE SPIRIT AND THE CITY.

Booze history is murky. What does exist are many manifests and other documents from cargo ships moving between Peru and California that note the arrival of pisco, even before the Gold Rush. Remember, California spoke Spanish and the Viceroyalty of New Spain was a geo-graphic cousin to the Viceroyalty of Peru—they shared a culture, and with it, their tastes in cuisine and drink. As vineyards had existed in Peru since the 1530s, wine and pisco had long been part of the culture of the Pacific. So, when San Francisco boomed, with its success came the popularity of pisco, exotic and mixable and unlike any other tipple at the time.

WHERE WAS THE BEGINNING OF COCKTAIL HISTORY IN NORTH-ERN CALIFORNIA?

A full-on culture of cocktails didn't exist in London or New York in 1849 because there wasn't the economic capacity for it. Whereas in the richest city in the history of the world—San Francisco, from 1849 to 1893—every ship in the world stormed our harbors, their hulls thick with Champagne and Cognac and rum and pisco and more! Because they could. Bars bought in heavy, bartenders were allowed to mix and play because their patrons were thousands of miles away from their families and filthy rich. Why not have a ridiculous blast of a time? And so the culture of experimental, creative cocktails was born. And that's the uniquely San Franciscan tradition to which I belong.

Further, other cities with cocktail history began with a mixed record, covering up bathtub gin and gunpowder whiskey. They had to sling cocktails to make nasty booze passable. Not so in San Francisco, which began with the finest ingredients, created culinary concoctions, and then served the most expensive cocktails in the world. And it all started near what is Chinatown today, around Portsmouth Square, along Kearny Street when the water reached what is now Montgomery Street in today's Financial District, downtown San Francisco.

WHO ARE SOME OF THE MOST IMPORTANT FIGURES IN THE CITY'S EARLY COCKTAIL HISTORY THAT READERS SHOULD KNOW ABOUT?

There are plenty, in the 19th and 20th centuries, whether it's Harry Johnson or Trader Vic. In *Drinking the Devil's Acre*, I included both a chronology of persons and events significant to San Francisco's cocktail history plus I took the liberty of tracing my genealogy behind the stick, my mentors and theirs all the way back to Jerry Thomas—the founder of American mixology. I mean, there's no DNA, per se! But I take great pride in representing an unbroken chain of barkeeps who knew and worked for the greats of every previous generation all the way back to the 1850s.

FINALLY, FOR YOU PERSONALLY, ANY FAVORITE STORIES FROM YOUR UNIQUE POSITION HAVING SPENT MANY YEARS WORKING AT BARS AND RESTAURANTS AND RESEARCHING THEM?

We are here to live and celebrate our lives, and the saloon is the most human of conventions, a creative communal invention of intoxication and delight. San Francisco wouldn't be what it is without its vibrant history of drinking, and I'll add, neither would living.

· GOLD MOUNTAIN ·

DUGGAN MCDONNELL

McDonnell selected a California history-inspired cocktail to share for this collection. When enjoying this, make sure to think of our golden hills and the bright orange poppies (our state flower) that cover those hills in early spring.

GLASSWARE: Old Fashioned glass

GARNISH: Orange peel

- 1½ oz. California-produced rye whiskey
- ½ oz. California-produced brandy
- ½ oz. Coconut Syrup
- 1 bar spoon California Poppy Liqueur
- 2 dashes Angostura Bitters
- 2 dashes cacao bitters

1. Combine all of the ingredients in a mixing glass with ice, stir, and strain into an Old Fashioned glass over a large globe of ice.

2. Garnish with an expressed orange peel.

COCONUT SYRUP: Combine equal parts sugar and commercial coconut water in a saucepan over medium heat and stir until the sugar completely dissolves. Let cool and store.

HOW TO DRINK LIKE A SAN FRANCISCAN

First off, it's not Frisco. And Californians don't refer to the Golden State as "Cali," nor do we use "Golden State," except when referring to the Warriors.

Have a favorite Herb Caen quote in your back pocket. The great *San Francisco Chronicle* writer was arguably our city's most prominent voice for the 20th century. He was also our most prominent voice for discussing martinis. If someone says Herb Caen liked going to this bar—go.

Enjoy, or at least act like you enjoy, Fernet Branca. If a bartender does a shot with you, it will likely be this menthol-packed digestif. If not, it's probably their favorite mezcal.

Speaking of shots, if a bartender is wearing a Pin Project pin that means they are not drinking alcohol that day. Please don't pressure them to take a shot with you.

Anchor Steam & the Giants—that's basically Montana to Rice. Enjoy the pairing at any bar during the game. Or at the game!

Speaking of drinking at a Giants game, it's our favorite outdoor bar. Be a local and go where there is better beer at cheaper prices—in the Public House restaurant at 24 Willie Mays Plaza (you can carry them to your seats).

Embrace the old and new bars, and different neighborhoods. That's what makes San Francisco so great. Check in with the Buena Vista's Irish Coffee (see page 43) and Tommy's (see page 44), while also pursuing the latest and greatest.

Discuss dating apps, tech unicorn companies, or the latest, greatest tech gadgets. Yes, it's a very San Franciscan thing to do. But try not to talk about gentrification—it's the buzzword that always gets a heated debate going in this city.

Drink local spirits! When you see a local distillery on the menu, seriously consider getting that drink. We're spoiled with such great distilleries here.

It's very okay to start happy hour on the early side. Weekend Bloody Marys/beer/mimosas can begin before or after morning coffee. We're an active morning city, not a late-night city.

SAN FRANCISCO

CLASSIC COCKTAILS

PISCO PUNCH

MAI TAI

IRISH COFFEE

TOMMY'S MARGARITA

MARTINEZ

SAN FRANCISCO COCKTAIL

HOUSE CAPPUCCINO

CLASSIC MARTINI

CHARTREUSE SWIZZLE

TONY NEGRONI

BOOTHBY COCKTAIL

CABLE CAR

B efore we jump into today's cocktail renaissance, let's pay homage to twelve classics that define San Francisco cocktails. Whether you're visiting for the first time or you've lived here for decades, it's pretty much mandatory to at least *know* about these drinks. The first five are important parts of San Francisco's core history—and hopefully will be enjoyed by many generations in the future. The others have been instrumental in shaping the history of shaking, stirring, and drinking cocktails by the Bay, plus a "signature" drink that technically is famous yet actually doesn't really exist in San Francisco. I'll explain in a moment.

· PISCO PUNCH ·

COMSTOCK SALOON

One of San Francisco's most historic locally invented cocktails somehow still isn't an easily found drink around the city. In fact, I'd venture to guess that the majority of local bar-goers have never even heard of it. The bar in San Francisco to get the definitive Pisco Punch is Comstock Saloon in North Beach (a vintage saloon from The Absinthe Group with classic drinks and the highest quality of ingredients). Comstock is just a few blocks from where the drink was invented by Duncan Nichol at The Bank Exchange, a saloon located along what previously was the Bay's waterfront and where a little landmark called the Transamerica Pyramid stands today. City cocktail history doesn't get more fun than that! If you can find some Small Hand Foods Pineapple Gum Syrup, this is a wonderfully easy recipe for bringing a dash of San Francisco history to your home bar. Just accept the fact that you'll have to improvise the Nichol Juice. As The Absinthe's Group's Jonny Raglin says: "I make the secret ingredient and nobody has the recipe except me. It is common knowledge that the key ingredient is Makrut lime leaves but there are a number of other things in this tincture. It is called Nichol Juice as a nod to Duncan Nichol, who invented the drink in the 19th century here in the city. He took the recipe to his grave."

- 2 oz. pisco
- 1 oz. fresh lemon juice
- ¾ oz. Small Hand Foods Pineapple Gum Syrup
- 3-4 dashes of Nichol Juice

1. Combine all ingredients in a cocktail shaker with ice, shake vigorously, and double strain into a flip cup over a single medium cube.

2. Garnish with a lemon twist.

· MAI TAI ·

TRADER VIC'S

There is some debate over where and when the mai tai was created, between Don the Beachcomber and Trader Vic's, pitting SoCal against NorCal in the cocktail version of the Dodgers-Giants rivalry.

In the eyes of San Francisco cocktail history, it was Trader Vic Bergeron who invented the mai tai while behind the bar of his Oakland restaurant in 1944. He threw together these ingredients to create a new rum drink, added a lime shell for color, and served it to two friends visiting from Tahiti. One of them, Carrie Guild, according to Trader Vic's lore, took a sip and replied, "Mai Tai—Roa Ae." Translated from Tahitian, that means, "Out of this world—the best." And there you have the inspiration for the cocktail name.

Nowadays, it's fairly easy to find the Trader Vic's syrups needed to make this recipe. Rock candy syrup is always the curveball of the equation since it's kind of like simple syrup and kind of not. To complete *the* Trader Vic's Mai Tai, however, it's imperative to have it.

Of course, many drinkers have visions of tropical juices and pineapple garnishes when they think of mai tais. There is nothing wrong with those renditions, but that is not what the cocktail originally intended to be or, depending on your viewpoint, actually is. Trader Vic's is now on the waterfront in Emeryville, right next to Oakland, so you can order a Trader Vic's Mai Tai while gazing out at the South Pacific . . .well, you're looking at the Bay, which leads to the Golden Gate, which then means the islands of the South Pacific are only a few thousand miles beyond that.

GLASSWARE: Mai tai glass

GARNISH: Mint and lime shell

- 2 oz. Jamaican rum
- ¾ oz. orange curacao
- ½ oz. Trader Vic's Orgeat Syrup
- ¼ oz. fresh lime juice
- ¼ oz. Trader Vic's Rock Candy Syrup
- Juice of half a lime (reserve spent lime shell)

1. Combine all of the ingredients in a cocktail shaker with crushed ice, shake vigorously, and pour into the glass.

2. Garnish with mint and spent lime shell.

· IRISH COFFEE ·

THE BUENA VISTA

The well-told story (and the rare non-murky classic cocktail origin story) of this Ghirardelli Square area saloon's iconic specialty dates back to 1952, when travel writer Stanton Delaplane asked The Buena Vista's owner, Jack Koeppler, to replicate some supposedly amazing "Irish coffee" drink from the airport in Shannon, Ireland. Yes, it's a world-renowned drink from an airport! After lots of research and development before "R&D" really was a term (it even involved San Francisco mayor-dairy owner George Christopher in the search for the perfect cream), the drink and its 6 oz. glass mug became the new house specialty for an establishment that had already been around since the early 20th century. Thousands of Irish Coffees are still served weekly at The Buena Vista, where you can find a row of mugs always lined up on the bar.

GLASSWARE: Irish Coffee mug

- 6 oz. hot coffee
- 2 sugar cubes
- 1½ oz. Tullamore D.E.W. Irish Whiskey

- Lightly whipped whipping cream, for topping

1. Fill the mug with hot water to preheat, then empty.

2. Pour coffee into the mug, drop in two sugar cubes, add whiskey, and stir.

3. Top with a collar of whipped cream by pouring gently over a spoon.

· TOMMY'S MARGARITA ·

TOMMY'S MEXICAN RESTAURANT

I've seen the Tommy's Margarita recipe on cocktail menus on four continents and I'm almost certain that the other three have cocktail bars serving it as well—even Antarctica. San Francisco's most renowned cocktail creation isn't even a cocktail that was invented in the city. But it was perfected in San Francisco.

It's a pilgrimage for every cocktail drinker to go to the humble source of what is universally considered the ideal margarita. While most destinations with such an enormous global following tend to be flashy and happy to let you know how famous they are, Tommy's Mexican Restaurant on busy Geary Boulevard in the oh so diverse Outer Richmond neighborhood is nothing like that. It's a humble place owned by the Bermejo family that has been a city favorite for Mexican cuisine (specifically from the Bermejo's native Yucatán) since Tommy (Tomas) and his wife Elmy opened the restaurant in 1965.

A few decades after opening, their son Julio shaped Tommy's into a spectacular destination for studying and sipping the four kinds of premium 100% agave tequila—blanco, reposado, añejo, extra añejo (along with joven, which is a blend of reposado and blanco)—and he also created the margarita recipe heard 'round the world. There are three ingredients in this margarita (and most other versions) and each one matters critically:

Fresh lime juice.

100% agave tequila.

Agave nectar instead of an orange liqueur (or even worse, a commercial sour mix).

And, it goes without saying that this margarita—THE Tommy's Margarita—shall never be blended. Salt on the rim is up to you, but the three key components championed by Julio Bermejo and what you'll see shaken and served each day at Tommy's, cannot be negotiated. There's a reason this is the world's gold standard for margaritas.

GLASSWARE: Rocks glass
GARNISH: Salt rim, optional

- **2 oz. 100% agave tequila**
- **1 oz. fresh lime juice**
- **½ oz. agave nectar**

1. Rim the glass with salt, if desired.

2. Combine all of the ingredients in a cocktails shaker with ice, shake vigorously, and strain into the glass.

· MARTINEZ ·

MIMINASHI

Nowadays, Martinez (the city) in the East Bay's Contra Costa County is best known for the refineries that you see from the freeway (and some unfortunate fires at those refineries). A century and a half ago, however, Martinez was a major stop between San Francisco and California's Gold Country to the east in the foothills of the Sierra Nevada Mountains. The cocktail world loves to debate whether Jerry Thomas invented the Martinez cocktail in San Francisco for a traveler heading to Martinez or if the drink actually hails from its namesake city, or is neither true? Was it then adapted for the martini? Did the martini actually come first? The debates will never end. There is no debate, though, that it's a wonderful classic cocktail and will always be a fun part of San Francisco folklore.

For this recipe, I crossed the Carquinez Bridge from Martinez to Napa where Miminashi's Bar Director Andrew Salazar offered his take on the Gold Rush-era classic. He made sure to remind me that the high amount of vermouth is not a typo—the original has a larger amount of vermouth than gin. Unfortunately, Miminashi closed in late 2020, but this cocktail lives on.

GLASSWARE: Cocktail glass
GARNISH: Lemon peel

- 1 ½ oz. sweet vermouth
- 1 oz. Old Tom-style gin
- 1 bar spoon maraschino liqueur
- 1 dash Angostura Bitters
- 2 dashes orange bitters

1. Combine all of the ingredients in a mixing glass full of ice, stir, and strain into the glass.

2. Garnish with lemon peel.

· SAN FRANCISCO COCKTAIL ·

SPIRIT WORKS DISTILLERY

The Singapore Sling, the Manhattan—those classic cocktails evoke a sense of place correctly. The San Francisco cocktail? Very few bartenders, and even fewer drinkers, have ever heard of this peculiar cocktail with our city as its namesake. Nobody can really agree on its history, nor can they agree on its ingredients other than that it is based on sloe gin, which in itself is very rare to see on cocktail menus in San Francisco. Go figure. I don't recall ever seeing the cocktail on a menu in San Francisco. This is *San Francisco Cocktails*, however, so I'd be remiss not to include our namesake drink. With sloe gin as my guiding ingredient, I asked Spirit Works Distillery's Ashby Marshall if she'd ever heard of this cocktail, since the Sebastopol distillery is the Bay Area's source for outstanding sloe gin. Here is the recipe that she sent me. I'd love to make this cocktail one of San Francisco's favorite drinks.

GLASSWARE: Coupe
GARNISH: Maraschino cherry

- 1 oz. Carpano Antica Sweet Vermouth
- 1 oz. Dolin Dry Vermouth
- 1 oz. Spirit Works Sloe Gin
- 1 dash Bitter Girl Batch One Orange Bitters

1. Combine all of the ingredients in a mixing glass with ice, stir, and strain into the glass.

2. Garnish with maraschino cherry.

· HOUSE CAPPUCCINO ·

CREATED FOR TOSCA CAFE, 2013

As of press time during the COVID-19 crisis, North Beach's century-old Tosca Cafe had just reopened with a new ownership team and the promise of the House Cappuccino on the menu once guests could visit the restaurant. Seven years earlier, the bar/restaurant had another ownership change and brought in cocktail maestro Isaac Shumway to run the bar program. He took one of the city's signature cocktails, which dates back to Prohibition (it tasted like a boozy, watery cappuccino when I first tried it a decade ago), and completely rejuvenated it for today's crowd.

GLASSWARE: Irish Coffee mug

- **2 cups cream**
- **3-4 oz. Cap Chocolate Mix**
- **½ oz. bourbon**
- **½ oz. Cognac**

1. Preheat a tempered hot beverage glass with boiling hot water.

2. Heat cream on the stove or with an espresso wand until it's very hot. Froth with a cappuccino wand or cappuccino mixer wand until you have a nice cappuccino foam.

3. Stir or shake Cap Mix, pour into a pot and heat on the stove or with an espresso wand until very hot.

4. Pour chocolate Cap Mix in heatproof glass, leaving room for the liquor and foam.

5. Add bourbon and Cognac.

6. With a spoon, top the House Cappuccino with the cream foam. Pour a little of the cream on top of the foam at the end and serve.

CAP CHOCOLATE MIX: In a large bowl, combine 1 quart Chocolate Ganache, 12 oz. hot water, 12 oz. organic milk, and 4 oz. Vanilla Syrup and mix well.

CHOCOLATE GANACHE: Add 24 oz. heavy cream to a saucepan over medium-high heat and bring to a simmer; when it begins to simmer turn off the burner. In a large bowl, combine 12 oz. chopped unsweetened dark chocolate and ½ teaspoon salt. Pour the heated cream over the chocolate, let sit for 5 minutes, and then stir until well mixed.

VANILLA SYRUP: Split a vanilla bean in half and scrape out the seeds; reserve both the pod and the seeds. Combine 1 cup water and 1 cup sugar in a saucepan over medium-high heat and bring to a simmer, stirring to dissolve the sugar. When the mixture begins to simmer, add the scraped vanilla pod and the seeds, remove the pan from the heat, and let steep until cool. Strain and store.

· CLASSIC MARTINI ·

SELBY'S

At this point, I'm not going to add anything more to the martini-Martinez discussion. After thinking about all of the possible stories of the cocktail's origin, I kind of just want a stiff drink! And the martini cart at Selby's definitely accomplishes that. The Bacchus Management Group's newest restaurant, at the edge of Redwood City and Atherton on the Peninsula, offers a martini that gets resolutely to the point—there isn't even any stirring involved. Bacchus' founding partner Tim Stannard wanted "the coldest martini on the West Coast" and he found a way to do that by taking recently frozen gin and immediately pouring it in the vermouth-rinsed glass. Of course, this means that there is no ice dilution that stirring would normally provide, which means that a three-martini lunch of this rendition might actually feel like a four-martini lunch.

GLASSWARE: Chilled cocktail glass
GARNISH: Olive, lemon twist, or onion

- ⅔ oz. chilled dry vermouth   • 4 oz. frozen gin

1. Swirl the inside of the chilled cocktail glass with vermouth.

2. Pour the gin directly into the glass and garnish with olive and lemon twist, or onion (in the case of a Gibson).

· CHARTREUSE SWIZZLE ·

CLOCK BAR

While the classic cocktails of San Francisco all were created in the middle of the 20th century or earlier, the most iconic 21st century cocktail from our fair city is the Chartreuse Swizzle. It's very simple, yet so profound. Swizzle (the tropics!) and Green Chartreuse (herbal, tangy, made by Carthusian monks in a secluded part of the French Alps) come together for this drink that is crushable and also an eye-brow-raising curiosity. It's the invention of Marco Dionysos, one of the key figures of the modern cocktail movement. He's a bit of an elusive figure these days, recently working at Smuggler's Cove and currently can be found some days at ABV.

Before inventing the Chartreuse Swizzle, Dionysos had a strong impact in the late 1990s at Absinthe Brasserie & Bar in Hayes Valley. He was "the first *technically* amazing bartender I ever saw," says Bay Area cocktail legend Scott Beattie. "[The Ginger Rogers cocktail] was one of the first not-sweet cocktails I had ever had. It changed my whole perspective on drinks. He was also an incredibly fast bartender. He had created this menu at Absinthe, which had about 40 kinds of resurrected classic cocktails, and the Ginger Rogers was one of them. I was just blown away that there were 40 drinks, none of which I had heard of, and this guy could make them like lightning speed. And they were delicious, with awesome garnishes. The guy was so fast and he'd be talking the whole time too."

A few years later, Dionysos created this drink by Union Square at the Westin St. Francis' beautiful Clock Bar, and the cocktail can now be found on menus all over the world.

GLASSWARE: Tall swizzle

- **1½ oz. Green Chartreuse**
- **1 oz. pineapple juice**
- **¾ oz. fresh lime juice**
- **½ oz. Velvet Falernum**

1. Combine all of the ingredients in the glass over pebble ice and swizzle with a bar spoon until the glass is frosted. Add more pebble ice if needed to fill glass for serving.

· TONY NEGRONI ·

POGGIO

San Francisco didn't invent the Negroni, of course. Yet, for some reason, it is often cited as the go-to classic cocktail for many, many San Francisco drinkers. Perhaps it's because of San Francisco's affection for Italy's culture and cuisine? Maybe it's because San Francisco gravitates to bitter flavors, as proven by the city's close connection to Fernet Branca? It also could be because San Francisco has been instrumental in the recent "Negroni Week" charity promotion, where for one week each year bars all around the country come up with creative takes on the Negroni with proceeds benefiting a charitable cause.

Regardless of why we love Negronis, it's just important to know that San Francisco truly goes wild for them. And who better to get our classic Negroni recipe from than Tony Negroni himself, Tony DiIorio, a longtime fixture behind the bar at Sausalito's Californian-Italian trattoria, Poggio.

GLASSWARE: Rocks glass

GARNISH: Orange peel, if serving up, or orange slice, if serving on the rocks

- 1 oz. Bombay Sapphire Gin
- 1 oz. Campari
- 1 oz. Carpano Antica Vermouth

1. Combine all of the ingredients in a cocktail shaker with cracked ice, shake vigorously, and strain into a chilled glass or over cubed ice.

2. Garnish with orange peel twist or orange slice, depending on how you choose to serve the drink.

· BOOTHBY COCKTAIL ·

THE HOUSE OF SHIELDS

I f you have "Cocktail" as your nickname, then you probably deserve a cocktail named for you. Along with Jerry Thomas, "Cocktail" William T. Boothby is the most legendary of early San Francisco bartenders, a man who seems almost larger-than-life when you read about how he was one of the biggest celebrities in San Francisco in the early years of the 20th century. His namesake cocktail is a Manhattan with a Champagne float and nobody does it better than bartender Shanti DeLuca and his team at The House of Shields, a legendary old bar now owned by Eric Passetti and Dennis Leary (who also run several fuss-free Financial District bars and breakfast-and-lunch sandwich take-out spots).

The House of Shields has enough history to fill a novel. It opened in 1908—two years after the city's big earthquake and fire, and the year that Boothby published the third edition (the one still used today) of his cocktail book, according to David Wondrich's must-read piece about Boothby at Liquor.com. The downtown bar is next to the Palace Hotel, where Boothby could be found working for much of his career. Supposedly, The House of Shields has a secret passageway to the hotel, but the bar won't tell you if that's true or not. When the bar was 15 years old, President Warren G. Harding died of a heart attack at the Palace Hotel (at least that's what the "official" reporting said). Some wonder, though, if the President really did die in the hotel . . .or possibly at The House of Shields. Lots of mysteries, lots of history, lots of classic cocktails to enjoy at one of San Francisco's truly great bars.

- 2 oz. 100-proof rye
- ¾ oz. Carpano Antica Formula Sweet Vermouth
- 2 dashes Angostura Bitters
- Float of brut sparkling wine

1. Combine all of the ingredients in a mixing glass with ice, stir, and strain into the glass. Stir ingredients with ice.

2. Add sparkling wine float and garnish with the cherry.

· BOOTHBY COCKTAIL ·

MIMINASHI

Two Boothby cocktails? Readers, I'm giving you a bonus Boothby recipe because I'm a big fan of seeing different takes on classics and was very intrigued by Andrew Salazar's addition of orange bitters. Give it a try—compare and contrast to The House of Shield's version. Besides, you probably have lots of Champagne left for more floats.

GLASSWARE: Stemmed cocktail glass

GARNISH: Cherries

- 1½ oz. rye
- ¾ oz. sweet vermouth
- 2 dashes Angostura Bitters
- 2 dashes orange bitters
- Champagne, to top

1. Combine all of the ingredients in a mixing glass with ice, stir, and strain into the glass.

2. Top with the Champagne until the glass is filled to just below the rim. Garnish with cherries.

MIMINASHI'S ROLODEX-O-COCKTAILS

Bar Director Andrew Salazar creates some of the most exciting new cocktails in the Napa Valley and the whole Bay Area. That doesn't mean, however, that he has brushed aside the importance of older cocktails. In fact, it's quite the contrary. In late 2017, Salazar unveiled a Rolodex of beloved and oft-ignored or forgotten cocktails. It's a brilliant concept to bundle all of these cocktails together Rolodex-style for fun, easy browsing.

In Salazar's words: "The reason for implementing the Rolodex was multi-fold. One of the biggest reasons was to gently encourage and suggest to our clientele a relatively concise list of drinks worth imbibing. I had anticipated that I would be making a wide array of cocktails for our guests, yet they seemed to be sticking to our house cocktails. While on the one hand, it was gratifying to see our featured cocktails being so well received, I was a bit puzzled as to why we weren't getting much in the way of classic/popular drink calls.

"In addition to being a good conversation piece, it was a bold declaration about our ambition and commitment toward establishing a vibrant cocktail culture in the heart of wine country. We wanted to be the standard-bearer for this objective.

"The cocktail Rolodex provided a practical study guide for wine/beverage professionals of all stripes. I worked with a similar application at a previous bar, but it was something reserved for the staff. A front-facing expanded cocktail list is a way to attract other bartenders, sommeliers, and cocktail enthusiasts to join us, have a great time, and spread to good word about what we were doing at Miminashi."

MIMINASHI
耳なし芳一
COCKTAIL ROLODEX

· CABLE CAR ·

TONY ABOU-GANIM

Of course, San Francisco needs a drink named after its iconic cable cars. As you might guess, it is related to a traditional sidecar except the pivotal difference is their base (this one is rum; sidecar is cognac). Sidecars also have lemon juice, while the lemon component for a Cable Car is from Lemon Sour.

If you've ridden the Powell-Hyde cable car in San Francisco, you've drifted by the Sir Francis Drake Hotel near Union Square, where the Starlight Room (now Lizzie's Starlight) resides 21 stories up atop the hotel. It opened in 1928 and through the decades has almost always been one of San Francisco's swankiest lounges for dancing, parties, live music, and, of course, cocktails. When the lounge was losing its edge in the mid-1990s, famed city bon vivant/restaurateur Harry Denton was brought in by the Kimpton Hotel Group to save the night—and he did so, with lots of help from the bar manager that he hired: Tony Abou-Ganim. His Cable Car cocktail quickly became a staple at the lounge, high above the historic cable car rolling by every few minutes on Powell Street.

GLASSWARE: Chilled cocktail glass
GARNISH: Cinnamon/sugar rim and orange spiral

- 1½ oz. Captain Morgan Spiced Rum
- ¾ oz. Marie Brizard Orange Curacao
- 1½ oz. Lemon Sour

1. Rim the glass with a mixture of equal parts cinnamon and superfine sugar.

2. Combine all of the ingredients in a mixing glass with ice, stir, and strain into the cocktail glass.

4. Garnish with an orange spiral.

LEMON SOUR: In a squeeze bottle, combine 2 parts fresh lemon juice with 1 part simple syrup and mix well.

VIRGINIA MILLER
WRITER, HISTORIAN,
WORLD'S 50 BEST ACADEMY CHAIR:
WEST USA & WEST CANADA

Trust me on this—nobody follows the restaurants and bars world of the Bay Area like Virginia Miller. Long before the internet became saturated with people claiming to be experts, Miller was already learning from the wizards of the crafts firsthand and has been writing about it for Bay Area residents. Miller preceded me as the Bay Area's editor for Zagat, which is how I first met her. Since that introduction, I've *tried* to bring her scholarly view of the food and drinks world to every restaurant, every bar, every interview, every winery, every *anything* I visit for work purposes. Miller's resume includes way too many publications for me to feature here. For cocktail stories, you've surely read her work at *Liquor.com*, and in *Gin Magazine UK* and *Distiller Magazine*. Born in Oklahoma, and raised in New Jersey and Southern California, the Bay Area is now the longtime, beloved home for this globetrotting writer.

Virginia and I (and my dog Deja) chatted at The Richfield in the Inner Richmond while enjoying another subject that we're both huge geeks about—Italian espresso drinks.

ON THE RENAISSANCE DAYS OF THE EARLY 2000S . . .

Those were just great days to come up. Those were great days for me to develop my palate because it was just master after master after pioneer after pioneer. People that were doing things that no one in the country had done yet.

Destino has been around since the 90s [Author's note: it closed during the pandemic, hoping to move to a new location]. That was a full-on pisco bar. Gaston Acurio's first restaurant outside of Latin America was here and that's over 10 years old now and *that* was a full pisco bar. We've always been a pisco town. Again, all these spirits that were not even trending in New York were trending here long before. You can trace it all.

Chartreuse was also popular here before anywhere else. I used to go to these Chartreuse gong shows at 15 Romolo, like 15 years ago. It used to be like a talent show where they literally had a giant gong. We would come and people were like "You're in or out!" *American Idol* style. They would hit the gongw if you're out, and we would all do shots of Green Chartreuse. This is going back so far that it was cheap because nobody else was drinking it.

When I was the critic at the *Guardian* (2008-2013), I did a cover story on San Francisco's top fifty bars. I don't remember exactly what year that was, maybe 2010, and by that point we were nuts. I could hardly even narrow it down to fifty. I narrowed it down to seventy-five and then wrestled for days on the twenty-five I had to cut. It has quadrupled and quadrupled since then. But, it was that vibrant then, when I could easily name a top 100. Easily. And that was when many cities were just getting started. The difference with other cities is we keep pioneering. We keep pushing those boundaries because the palate is already twenty steps ahead. And it's the same with food. We start so many of those trends and we don't get credit. It happens time and time again. It's always attracted that level of educated palate. When you've attracted that many people, then they all feed off of each other.

And the camaraderie is good here in the bar scene. That's the other thing—the borders are looser here. That raises the standard for everybody and people are willing to share their techniques. It's one of the most influential, highly trend-setting cities but operates like a small city, so it keeps that camaraderie a lot of small cities brag about. It's had that here in the bar scene since the beginning.

ON WHAT MAKES SAN FRANCISCO'S BAR SCENE SO UNIQUE . . .
San Francisco goes after "all the rest." Of course, we do gin, whiskey, and all the big guys, but we go way beyond that. We already had that palate for bitter, that palate for oxidation. San Francisco is always that pioneering "What's next?" kind of palate. What's funky, what's unusual, what hasn't been tried?

OLD HAUNTS

While this book is *slightly* more focused on the "craft" side of the cocktail bar spectrum, don't get me wrong, San Francisco loves a great dive bar, and low-key historical bars, too. Some days you want to forgo drinks with tinctures and five-ingredient syrups in favor of joints with plenty of character that bar concepts can't simply "create." Pardon the expression, but you can take a deep *dive* into the many historical "legacy" bars around the city by visiting the comprehensive map created by *San Francisco Heritage* on their website. It's an incredibly important project trying to protect older bars, seeing how the younger generation *generally* tends to be skipping these bars for flashier newer ones, plus there's always the problem of skyrocketing rent prices that these bars face (real estate prices are always a sticky subject in San Francisco). It's a tough combination and we need to protect these pieces of San Francisco's fun-loving, good times rolling past. Everyone has some personal favorites in this genre and you can't really judge who is more historic than whom (or necessarily expect the most refined, exquisite cocktail perfection). They are critical parts of what makes San Francisco such a unique city. But if you want eight to start your exploring itinerary, I'd steer you to:

Gino & Carlo's (North Beach)

Li-Po (Chinatown)

Lone Palm (Mission)

The Page (NoPa)

Shotwell's (Mission)

Spec's (North Beach)

Tony Nik's (North Beach)

Vesuvio (North Beach)

THE MISSION, DOGPATCH,

POTRERO HILL & BERNAL HEIGHTS

CHARTREUSE SLUSHY	THE CHURCH
EGGNOG PUNCH	ITALIAN GREYHOUND
IN THE PINES, UNDER THE PALMS	SONG REMAINS THE SAME
GARBAGE SLING!	BLACK SABBATH
SAM FLORES	MARNIE
PAMPLEMOUSSE AU POIVRE	PERFECT STRANGER
TOM & JERRY	AFTER THE GOLD RUSH
FORTUNATO'S REVIVER	PISCO SOUR
HOPSCOTCH	MR. KOTTER
SIDEWINDER	HOME IS WHERE THE HEAT IS
THE BEEHIVE	MEZCAL ALOE MOLE
	CARRIED AWAY

The southeast of San Francisco features two substantial hills, Bernal Heights and Potrero Hills, both of which boast stunning views and cute village-like main streets. Surrounding those hills and extending to the waterfront to the east are the Mission and Dogpatch neighborhoods. As the name suggests, the Mission is home to Mission Dolores. What the name doesn't suggest is that it is the greatest concentration of excellent cocktail bars in the city—and I'd even say in the entire country (sorry, East Village or DTLA). So many of the icons are there—ABV, True Laurel, Trick Dog, Elixir, Wildhawk, Beretta, and on and on. Come thirsty. The Mission is also San Francisco's main Latino neighborhood with many favorite taquerias and beautiful large-scale murals scattered throughout its dense blocks. To the east, the Dogpatch is often considered one of the last somewhat undeveloped frontiers of the very developed city. Historically, it had active docks and busy warehouses. You can still see that when walking around, except today there are spiffy new condos and an ever-growing number of notable bars and restaurants mixed amongst the industrial blocks and dilapidated piers.

· CHARTREUSE SLUSHY ·

THE MORRIS

This is owner Paul Einbund's interpretation of the Mamadetta, a drink served each year at the Santa Tecla Festival in Tarragona, Spain, and it's the quirky signature cocktail for Eibund's debut restaurant, The Morris, located between the Mission and Potrero Hill. Einbund is one of San Francisco's most talented sommeliers, so not surprisingly the wine program is as good as it gets. But, he's also a serious Chartreuse nerd, which explains the Chartreuse Slushy's importance at the restaurant (not to mention the wonderful collection of vintage Chartreuse at The Morris). So, you've got the best of the wine and Chartreuse worlds together to choose from for accompanying The Morris' signature smoked duck. We should also note that The Morris resides in the longtime home of Slow Club, one of the defining restaurants and bars of the 1990s and early 2000s.

GLASSWARE: Chartreuse snifter

- 2¼ oz. tart lemonade
- 1 oz. Green Chartreuse
- 2½ oz. palm syrup, or simple syrup

1. In a blender, combine all of the ingredients with ice and blend. Pour into the snifter.

LAZY BEAR

Guests at the lavish, irresistibly fun Lazy Bear "dinner parties" start with a cocktail reception in the upstairs Den. Many of the city's top chefs and bartenders have passed through the kitchen and bar of David Barzelay's trailblazing pop-up turned restaurant in the Mission. Otello Tiano is the restaurant's former bar director, and today continues to create some of the most exciting classic and inventive libations in the entire Bay Area at Single Thread in Healdsburg. In the spirit of being a communal fine-dining experience, Lazy Bear often serves punch bowl cocktail options (in addition to a host of other intricate creations). What is more festive than eggnog and punch?

GLASSWARE: **Punch bowl and punch glasses**

- **1 quart buttermilk**
- **2 quarts whole milk**
- **3 pints heavy cream**
- **24 oz. dark rum**
- **18 oz. VSOP Brandy**

- **3 teaspoons pumpkin spice**
- **6 eggs**
- **1½ cups sugar**
- **Salt, to taste**

1. In a large container, combine the buttermilk, milk, cream, rum, brandy, and pumpkin spice.

2. Separate egg yolks from egg whites.

3. Combine yolks and 1 cup sugar in the bowl of a stand mixer. Use the beater attachment and blend until vibrant yellow. Add egg mixture to the liquid mixture and whisk until incorporated.

4. Rinse out the stand mixer's bowl and then combine the egg whites with the remaining sugar. Use the whisk attachment and run until soft peaks form.

5. Fold the egg white mixture into the liquid mixture. Do this with only a bit of the egg whites at a time to create a more luscious texture when finished.

6. Chill before serving.

NICOLAS TORRES

It's hard to single out which San Francisco bar has the most *innovative* or *intricate* cocktails. In recent years, techniques like clarification and milk-washed or the idea of foraging, infusions, and bottling effervescent cocktails haven't exactly become clichés, but they're prevalent enough now to the point that you see them throughout this book. Nicolas Torres is a large reason for that, seeing how his meticulous style of cocktail design is indeed the city's standard for innovative, intricate drinks without gimmicks. During his tenure as bar manager for Lazy Bear, Torres created cocktails that were way ahead of the curve. He continues to push the techniques and ingredients envelope at True Laurel, which he and partner David Barzelay (Lazy Bear's chef-owner) opened in December 2017. Torres is a trailblazer for techniques—never flashy in the modernist style, but always seeing what could possibly add a new flavor layer or textural component. He is also a cocktail pioneer for his resolute desire to be resourceful with ingredients (basically no fruit peel or part of an herb goes untouched) and to evoke a sense of California place that is seen more in beer and wine than cocktails.

TRUE LAUREL

Rye whiskey and gin, tropics and forests—many different worlds combine in this unique masterpiece by Nicolas Torres at Lazy Bear's relaxed sibling, also in the Mission District. It's a perfect example of Torres's distinct style that emphasizes California nature and clever techniques for achieving new flavor dimensions.

"I wanted to make a twist on a local classic while keeping to our ethos of working with local produce," Torres says. "I decided to do a twist on a Martinez that utilized St. George Terroir Gin. This gin was already inspired by the native plant habitat of Mt Tamalpais. I had already been foraging redwood shoots for dishes and that seemed like a natural fit to introduce that Northern California essence to the drink. The pairing of coconut and pine came in a dream—I work too much—but it turned out to be a beautiful pairing. We decided to bring that flavor in on a new base and rye whiskey jumped out to us because the Martinez is always a great drink to introduce to whiskey drinkers that claim they don't like gin. It really came together!"

Torres also notes that at True Laurel these cocktails are bottled so each drink can sit with the redwood sprout for at least a day "to pick up the foresty flavors."

GLASSWARE: Rocks glass
GARNISH: Redwood or pine sprout

- ¾ oz. St. George Terroir Gin
- ¾ oz. Toasted Coconut Rye
- ¾ oz. Oliveros Vermouth
- ¼ oz. Luxardo Maraschino
  Liqueur
- ¼ oz. water
- 2 dashes Angostura Bitters
- Redwood or pine sprout

1. Combine all of the ingredients in a mixing glass with ice and stir.

2. Strain into a rocks glass and garnish with a redwood or pine sprout.

COCONUT RYE: Pour a liter of rye into a mason jar. In a saucepan, bring 2 healthy tablespoons of organic coconut oil to a low simmer. Pour a cup of coconut flakes in the oil and remove from heat. Stir and brown the flakes in the oil. Add the complete mixture to the mason jar while the oil is still in liquid form. Seal the jar, shake, and let sit for 10 minutes then shake again. Place the jar in the freezer overnight. The next day, fine strain for the finished product.

· GARBAGE SLING! ·

Rejiggered classic slings and creative new slings are two of the specialties at the Bon Vivants' imaginative Valencia Street sibling to Trick Dog. The drink incorporates ingredients that Bon Voyage! would ordinarily discard and compost.

GLASSWARE: Tall bamboo glass

- 2 oz. Tanqueray Rangpur Gin
- 1½ oz. Rice Milk Tepache
- ¾ oz. Penicillin Syrup
- ½ oz. fresh lemon juice
- 2 dashes Angostura Bitters

1. Combine all of the ingredients in a cocktail shaker with ice, shake vigorously, and double strain into a bamboo glass over crushed ice.

RICE MILK TEPACHE: In a large bowl, combine 2 cups Rice Milk with 2 cups Fermented Pineapple and whisk until incorporated. Strain through a chinois and add ⅓ cup Tempus Fugit Creme de Noyaux. Stir to combine and store.

RICE MILK: In a large bowl, combine 1 cup day-old cooked rice with 1 liter water and let sit for 10 minutes. Blend the rice and water until thoroughly incorporated and then strain through a chinois.

FERMENTED PINEAPPLE: In a large container with a lid, combine 2 pounds pineapple pieces (butts, cut off bits, skins—anything leftover), 1 liter water, and 8¾ oz. sugar and leave in the refrigerator to ferment.

PENICILLIN SYRUP: In a pot over medium-low heat, combine 500g granulated sugar, 500g honey, 400 ml water, 100 ml Ardbeg or Laphroaig 10 Scotch, 100g sliced ginger plus any ginger skin from previous projects, and 1 teaspoon salt and heat until just incorporated. Promptly remove from heat, and let stand 4 hours before straining and storing.

TRICK DOG

Don't ever get too attached to a favorite drink at Trick Dog since the menu rotates every six months. Please don't worry too much, though, because each menu in the bar's acclaimed history has had countless favorites that are already San Francisco cocktail legends. One of those cocktails is this spicy tequila and horchata drink from the ninth menu, the Trick Dog Mural Project, when the bar teamed up with fourteen local artists, including Sam Flores himself, to make fourteen murals around the city and name drinks after each artist. This is literally an artistic cocktail in more than one way.

GLASSWARE: Small clay pot
GARNISH: Orange wheel and lime wheel

- 1½ oz. Ocho Plata Tequila
- 1 oz. Ancho Reyes
- 2½ oz. Pear Cardamom Horchata
- ½ oz. fresh lime juice
- 1 dash Angostura Bitters

1. Combine all of the ingredients in a cocktail shaker, shake vigorously, and double strain into a food safe clay pot over ice.

2. Garnish with an orange wheel and lime wheel.

PEAR CARDAMOM HORCHATA: Preheat oven to 350°F. Place 3½ cinnamon sticks, 14 green cardamom pods, and a ¾ piece of nutmeg on a sheet pan and toast in the oven for 20 minutes. In a large container with a lid, combine 1.75 qt pear juice, 1 qt water, 4¼ cups jasmine rice, 1 lb. honey, 1 vanilla bean, peel of 1 small lime, and the toasted aromatics and let stand overnight at room temperature. Blend the mixture 1 quart at a time. Strain through an ultra-fine sieve bag, and subsequently strain through a chinois. Add 2 oz. cinnamon syrup for every 1 quart of horchata.

· PAMPLEMOUSSE AU POIVRE ·

ELIXIR

H. Joseph Ehrmann won the 2018 Cocktail of the Year award with this cocktail at the San Francisco World Spirits Competition. After trying its perfect balance of smoke, spice, and tanginess, you'll understand why.

GLASSWARE: Short glass or cocktail glass
GARNISH: Grapefruit peel cone with pink peppercorns rested on the rim (at the competition);
wide lemon twist sprinkled with pink peppercorns (at Elixir)

- 2 oz. mezcal (Del Maguey Vida is used at Elixir; the competition was won with Mezcal Banhez)
- 1 oz. Giffard Pamplemousse
- ½ oz. Marie Brizard Poivre de Sichuan, or housemade Elixir de Poivre Cordial
- ½ oz. fresh lemon juice
- 1 dash Bitter Truth Grapefruit Bitters

1. Combine all of the ingredients in a cocktail shaker with ice, shake vigorously, and strain into the glass.

2. Serve one of two ways: Short, over crushed ice and garnished with a sprinkle of pink peppercorns and a wide lemon twist (as prepared in Elixir); up into a cocktail glass with a grapefruit peel cone filled with pink peppercorns rested on the rim (as originally prepared).

ELIXIR DE POIVRE CORDIAL: Combine 8 oz. Stolen Heart Vodka (120 proof), 1 tablespoon pink peppercorns, ¼ teaspoon Sichuan peppercorns, and ½ teaspoon coriander seeds in a mason jar and let sit at room temperature for 24 hours. Strain and then mix with simple syrup at a 1:1 ratio.

· TOM & JERRY ·

ELIXIR

For a handful of days around Christmas, Elixir becomes *the* bar to visit for holiday drink classics. The most December chill-defeating of these drinks is the one and only Tom & Jerry. It's a hard drink to find anywhere because it's not trivial to make. Luckily, H. Joseph Ehrmann's recipe nicely breaks down the drink. Think of it as two parts: the batch, then the drink. Supposedly it's a specialty of Buffalo, New York, but my girlfriend's family (from Buffalo) had never even heard of this drink before I introduced them to the one from Elixir.

GLASSWARE: 12 oz. mug

GARNISH: Freshly grated nutmeg

- 8 jumbo eggs
- 1½ cups powdered sugar
- 1 teaspoon vanilla extract
- ½ teaspoon cream of tartar
- Hot water
- ¾ oz. rum
- ¾ oz. brandy
- 4-5 oz. frothed hot milk
- 1 (750 ml) bottle Appleton Estate Special Rum
- 1 (750 ml) bottle Sacred Bond Brandy

1. Separate the egg whites and yolks.

2. In a large mixing bowl, beat the yolks with the sugar and vanilla until thin.

3. In another bowl, combine the egg whites and cream of tartar and beat until stiff and form peaks that stand up; if they flop over, keep beating.

4. Fold the yolk mixture into the egg whites mixture and mix until the batter is thick, but light.

5. Preheat a 12 oz. mug with hot water and let rest. Discard the water and then add 4 oz. of the egg mixture to the mug.

6. Add the rum and brandy to the mug, top with frothed milk, and stir gently.

7. Garnish with freshly grated nutmeg and serve with a paddle or spoon.

· HOPSCOTCH ·

BLACKBIRD

Beer cocktails are increasingly trendy in San Francisco and we've seen frothy egg white-based sours forever. But, beer *and* egg whites? That is pretty rare. There is a lot going on in this cocktail created by Sean Riley in 2015, yet it's so simple to produce. It's another fantastic Blackbird classic.

GLASSWARE: Small rocks glass

- • **2 oz. Famous Grouse Scotch**
- • **½ oz. Gran Classico**
- • **¾ oz. egg white**
- • **¼ oz. agave syrup**
- • **1 oz. Moose Drool Brown Ale**

1. Combine all of the ingredients in a Boston shaker and dry shake.

2. Add ice, shake for 10 seconds, and fine strain into a chilled small rocks glass.

3. Express orange oils over drink and discard peel.

BREWER-AY AREA

Need a beer break from all the cocktails? You're in luck. The whole "craft beer" thing has swept across the Bay Area in the past decade with all the gusto of Karl the Fog coming in on a summer afternoon. It seems like there's a brewery in every town of the Bay Area (and usually in an out-of-the-way warehouse location). Anchor Brewing was founded in 1896, nearly faded into extinction but was turned into the first modern craft brewery in the 1960s, and deservedly remains the city's world-renowned beer icon today (now it's under different ownership than Anchor Distilling). You see and literally drink history when going on a tour of their Potrero Hill brewery. Russian River (Santa Rosa) and Lagunitas (Petaluma) are the modern legends of the hop-forward style that has ruled the 21st century. In the eyes of this author, who has been to more than his fair share of breweries, these are the ones in the Bay Area that have an excellent blend of quality and experience. Please visit many of the other great breweries, but I suggest starting with these eight.

Barebottle (Bernal Heights)—Endlessly creative and fun.

Blackhammer (SoMa) —Excellent variety, across-the-board high quality.

Cellarmaker (SoMa) —San Francisco's definitive place for IPAs.

Faction (Alameda) —The San Francisco skyline view alone is worth a trip and the beer happens to be excellent.

GravSouth (Cotati)—Best little brewery that the Bay Area doesn't really know about it.

The Rare Barrel (Berkeley)—Bay Area's sour beer leader.

Russian River —Pliny the Elder (and his younger sibling) need no introduction, being the Bay Area's most beloved modern beer.

Temescal (Oakland)—Best beer garden/brewery combination.

BLACKBIRD

At the edge of the Castro and the always-bustling Duboce Triangle area (a smorgasbord of transit stops, shopping, a popular bike route called "The Wiggle" and Duboce Park), Blackbird functions as so many great things—a gay bar, a locals bar for billiards, an intimate date bar, a serious cocktail bar, or a chill place for a beer. Opened in 2009, it was also one of the first in the city to make the sometimes overly complex world of high-quality cocktails much more approachable. It's amazing to look at this Brent Butler recipe from 2011 because it's the type of drink that hip new bars around the world today would serve. Blackbird served it a decade ago.

GLASSWARE: Swizzle glass
GARNISH: Lime twist

- 1 ½ oz. Partida Reposado Tequila
- ½ oz. Campari
- ½ oz. vanilla syrup
- ¾ oz. fresh lime juice
- ½ oz. ginger syrup
- 1 pinch salt

1. Combine all of the ingredients in a tall glass with crushed ice and swizzle until the glass is frosted.

2. Top with crushed ice and garnish with lime twist.

· THE BEEHIVE ·

THE BEEHIVE

It isn't easy to follow a legend and win a Super Bowl like Steve Young did after Joe Montana left the 49ers. That was close to the tall task given to The Beehive when it replaced Range, a restaurant that launched the careers of many top San Francisco bartenders and also helped put the Mission on the city's midscale/upscale dining map. Range's former chef/owner Phil West is now part of a formidable team, including star designer/contractor Steve Werney and one of the city's longtime favorite chefs, Arnold Eric Wong, that opened The Beehive (and also own or co-own The Treasury and The Third Rail). The Beehive looks to the glamorous, swinging, three martini-lunch era of the 60s for a modern-retro vibe in the revamped Range space. Its namesake cocktail by bar manager Emilio Salehi borrows from a classic Bee's Knees, but adds the subtle bite of ginger and the nostalgic Americana-evoking flavor profile (and the effervescence) of sarsaparilla root beer. It's a buzzy cocktail that absolutely deserves to be The Beehive's signature drink.

GLASSWARE: Collins
GARNISH: Lemon twist

- 1 oz. soda water
- 1½ oz. The Botanist Islay Dry Gin
- ¾ oz. fresh lemon juice
- ¾ oz. Ginger Solution
- ½ oz. Sarsaparilla-Infused Honey Syrup
- 2 dashes orange bitters
- 2 dashes Salt Solution

1. In a tall glass, pour 1 oz. of soda water.

2. Combine all of the other ingredients in a cocktail shaker with ice, shake vigorously, strain into the soda water, and add ice.

3. Garnish with a lemon twist.

GINGER SOLUTION: In a jar, combine equal parts hot water, evaporated cane sugar, and fresh ginger juice. Stir until sugar is fully dissolved.

SARSAPARILLA-INFUSED HONEY SYRUP: In a jar, combine 2 cups high-grade local honey, 1 cup hot water, 1 oz. Indian Sarsaparilla and stir to combine. Allow sarsaparilla to infuse for 24 hours before straining and storing in the refrigerator.

SALT SOLUTION: Combine 20g hot water with 1g salt. Stir until the salt is fully dissolved.

· THE CHURCH ·

LOCANDA

As I started this book, I never would have imagined that one of my favorite restaurants would be forced to close because of a global pandemic and subsequent shelter-in-place orders. Yet, here I am writing about The Church knowing that I won't get to try it at Locanda again. The restaurant was a beautiful ode to Rome by Craig and Annie Stoll, owners of the superb Delfina and Pizzeria Delfina. Along with terrific rustic Roman food, Locanda was San Francisco's definitive place to try Italian aperitivo-style cocktails. Many thanks to Bree Bojorquez and Annie Stoll for continuing to help me with this recipe even after the closure was announced. It is an honor that this book can make sure that The Church will always be around to help folks remember Locanda.

GLASSWARE: Double rocks glass
GARNISH: Orange ribbon

- 1 oz. Aperol
- 1 oz. City of London Gin
- 1 oz. fresh lemon juice
- ½ oz. Small Hands Foods Gum Syrup
- ½ oz. Cocchi Americano

1. Add all of the ingredients to a cocktail shaker with ice, shake vigorously, and double strain into double rocks glass over a large rock of ice.

2. Garnish with an orange ribbon.

· ITALIAN GREYHOUND ·

PRAIRIE

C hef and owner Anthony Strong is both one of our city's most eloquent voices for discussing subjects well beyond the restaurant industry, and one of our leading culinary talents. After leading the kitchens at Pizzeria Delfina and Locanda, he ventured out on his own with various pop-up and start-up models before opening his own live-fire driven restaurant in the Mission. Prairie's tiny bar focuses on Italian amaro and Japanese whisky, and always features this simple, wonderful aperitivo inspired by Strong's time living in Rome (when he was studying for Locanda's opening). During the COVID-19 pandemic, Prairie turned on a dime into the Prairie General Store, providing all kinds of essential goods for San Franciscans as major stores started running out of many kinds of foods and items like toilet paper. Sadly, Prairie also announced its permanent closure during the pandemic. So we raise our Italian Greyhound to Strong and his staff of this small, mighty, compassionate restaurant.

GLASSWARE: Rocks glass
GARNISH: Grapefruit wheel

- 1 oz. vodka
- ½ oz. Cappelletti
- ½ oz. Bruto Americano

- **Fresh grapefruit juice, to top**

1. Combine all of the ingredients, except the grapefruit juice, in a rocks glass with a giant ice cube, top with fresh-squeezed grapefruit juice, and stir.

2. Garnish with a grapefruit wheel.

· SONG REMAINS THE SAME ·

FOREIGN CINEMA

With a Fellini film playing on the courtyard's wall, twinkling lights over-head and excellent California meets the globe cuisine on the table, an evening (or brunch) at this Mission stalwart is about as magical as it gets in San Francisco. If I ever get married, I'd probably like to get married here—and I'm definitely not the only one who has said that. The atmosphere is so special that it's easy to forget how great the food and drinks are. Bryan Ranere created this scotch-based composition at the restaurant and named it for the 1976 Led Zeppelin behind-the-scenes concert film.

GLASSWARE: Coupe or cocktail glass
GARNISH: Citrus peel

- **2 oz. Ardbeg Scotch Whisky**
- **½ oz. Cherry Heering Liqueur**
- **½ oz. fresh lemon juice**
- **½ oz. Honey Simple Syrup**
- **2 drops Bittermens Orange Bitters**

1. Combine all of the ingredients in a cocktail shaker filled three-quarters with ice, shake for 15 seconds, and strain into a coupe or cocktail glass.

2. Garnish with the citrus peel.

HONEY SIMPLE SYRUP*: Combine ¼ cup orange blossom or other floral honey with ¼ cup water in a small saucepan over medium heat, bring to a simmer, stirring frequently, and cook for 2 to 3 minutes, until the honey dissolves completely. Let cool completely. Refrigerate the syrup in an airtight container for up to 2 weeks.

*Originally published in The Foreign Cinema Cookbook: Recipes and Stories Under the Stars.

· BLACK SABBATH ·

FOREIGN CINEMA

Named by Gail Izaguirre for a 1963 Italian horror trilogy (and made for a "hangover brunch service" that may have felt more than a bit brutal), this is a wonderful Italian-meets-SF cocktail with Sicilian blood orange liqueur, Prosecco, fresh Meyer lemon juice, and, of course, our good friend, Fernet Branca.

GLASSWARE: Collins

GARNISH: Lemon twist

- 1.2 oz. Fernet-Branca
- ¼ oz. Solerno Blood Orange Liqueur
- ½ oz. fresh Meyer lemon juice
- 3 oz. Prosecco

1. Fill a tall Collins glass with ice, add all of the ingredients, except the Prosecco, stir, and top with Prosecco.

2. To garnish, rub the lemon twist around the rim of the glass and then drop it into the drink.

· MARNIE ·

LASZLO

Laszlo is Foreign Cinema's adjacent bar right on Mission Street and features a completely different, equally impressive cocktail program (bar manager Nicky Beyries oversees both). Foreign Cinema opened in 1999 and Laszlo followed a year later, so both are now in their third decade of producing excellent cocktails with fresh juices and homemade syrups—yet they're rarely cited as one of the starting points for the city's modern cocktail movement. That's an oversight where perhaps my fellow cocktail historians have been too distracted by the fun atmosphere and cinematic joie de vivre at both establishments

And, as you may have guessed, all the drinks are nods to movies, directors, or characters. This cocktail is a bit more obscure, named for a 1964 Hitchcock film, and included on a themed menu titled "What's Wrong with Hitchcock's Women?" Per Laszlo, the menu "showcased a cocktail named for each one of Hitchcock's leading ladies and aimed to explore why these female figures were often despised and obsessed over by the auteur."

GLASSWARE: Small rocks glass or mug
GARNISH: Grated nutmeg and sprig of mint

- 2 oz. Absolut Elyx Vodka
- ¾ oz. Small Hand Foods Orgeat
- ¾ oz. fresh lime juice
- ¾ oz. Small Hand Foods Passion Fruit Syrup
- 1 pinch Maldon sea salt

1. Combine all of the ingredients in a cocktail shaker with ice, shake vigorously, and strain into small rocks glass or mug.

2. Top with crushed ice and microplane nutmeg on top. Add a small sprig of mint, if available.

LOLÓ

This unique and funky cocktail from Loló, a chic Mexican restaurant and cocktail bar on Valencia Street, is definitely among the best known in the city for one primary reason: goat's milk. Get past the goat novelty and it's ultimately a wonderful clarified milk punch that showcases a little spice punching into Lo-Fi's Dry Vermouth and the sweet-oxidation dual personality of Oloroso sherry.

GLASSWARE: Rocks glass
GARNISH: Lemon and lime twist

- 1½ oz. Ford's Gin
- ¾ oz. Lo-Fi Dry Vermouth
- ¼ oz. Lustau Dry Oloroso Sherry
- ½ oz. fresh lemon juice
- ¼ oz. fresh lime juice
- ½ oz. simple syrup
- ¼ oz. jalapeño brine
- 2 dashes celery bitters
- 1 pinch salt
- Goat's milk

1. Combine all of the ingredients, except the goat's milk, in a mixing glass and stir to combine.

2. Add the goat's milk, about one-fifth of the total amount in the mixing glass. Stir to combine and then strain through cheesecloth into a jar. Repeat the strain and then pour into a rocks glass over ice.

3. Garnish with lemon and lime twist.

· AFTER THE GOLD RUSH ·

HOLY WATER

Many of San Francisco's residential neighborhoods have one or a few high-level cocktails-and-craft beer bars that also function as the beloved casual neighborhood spot. They hit the best notes of an ambitious destination *and* being the beloved pub/saloon/dive/local watering hole. Holy Water in Bernal Heights is a great example of that. Here's the bar's longtime best seller, created by John Ottman: a play on the classic Gold Rush, which is of course a fitting classic cocktail to do a twist on in a city that gained much of its prominence because of the Gold Rush.

GLASSWARE: Rocks glass
GARNISH: Lime wheel

- 1½ oz. Old Grand Dad Bonded Bourbon
- ¾ oz. Small Hand Foods Pineapple Gum
- ½ oz. Rothman & Winter Apricot Liqueur
- ½ oz. fresh lime juice

1. Combine all of the ingredients in a cocktail shaker with ice, shake vigorously, and double strain into a rocks glass over ice.

2. Add a lime wheel for garnish.

· PISCO SOUR ·

MO-CHICA (POTRERO HILL)
AND LA COSTANERA (PACIFICA)

While the pisco punch is the city's most historical pisco cocktail, there is no doubt what the most frequently ordered and well-known pisco cocktail is. So, I asked the chef-owner of the Bay Area's leading Peruvian restaurant group, Carlos Altamirano of Altamirano Restaurant Group, to help us out and he kindly shared his recipe for the ratios and techniques that produce an ideal pisco sour.

GLASSWARE: Rocks glass

- • 2 oz. pisco
- • 1 oz. fresh lime juice
- • 1 oz. egg white
- • ¾ oz. simple syrup
- • Angostura Bitters, to top

1. Dry shake all of the ingredients, except the bitters, in a cocktail shaker until the egg white emulsifies with the rest of the liquids and becomes frothy, maybe five vigorous shakes or so. Then, handshake with ice for 9 to 12 seconds.

2. Strain into the glass and top with Angostura bitters.

· MR. KOTTER ·

Enrique Sanchez is undoubtedly one of San Francisco's present-day bar legends. After coming to study in San Francisco from his native Peru, Sanchez shifted to the cocktail industry, starting a career of nearly two decades as a bartender or bar manager for several important local restaurant cocktail programs, like La Mar, Beretta, and Arguello. Now he's running the show at Traci des Jardins's weeknights-only Dogpatch bar, School Night. That's right, it's open only on school nights. Luckily for us adults, this school involves the study of enjoying cocktails.

Now, cue the TV theme music, because here's Mr. Sanchez to tell you about Mr. Kotter: "We use one of our favorite tequilas in this cocktail, which is Tapatio. Tapatio is made in Jalisco but Tapatio is also a name you are called if you are from the region of Guadalajara. This drink is a combo of the classic margarita, which has orange liqueur, and the new age Tommy's Margarita, which has agave nectar. We are using both orange liqueur and agave nectar served over a hibiscus ice cube."

GLASSWARE: Old Fashioned glass
GARNISH: Orange wedge

- 2 oz. Tapatio Blanco Tequila
- ½ oz. Pierre Ferrand Dry Curaçao
- 1 oz. fresh lime juice
- ¼ oz. agave nectar

1. Combine all of the ingredients in a cocktail shaker with ice, shake vigorously, and double strain into an Old Fashioned glass over a Hibiscus Ice Cube.

2. Garnish with an orange wedge.

HIBISCUS ICE CUBES: Combine 2 liters water, 1 cup hibiscus flowers, and 1 whole orange peel in a saucepan over medium-high heat and bring to a boil. When the mixture boils, remove the pan from the heat and let steep for a couple hours before straining. Pour the strained liquid into 2x2 ice molds and freeze.

BESHARAM

Heena Patel is an absolute force of creativity and joyful exuberance, always smiling when cooking her unique style of Gujarati food or chatting with guests at her Dogpatch restaurant, Besharam. The cocktails at the restaurant wonderfully reflect the spirit of the food program, like in this mezcal-tamarind cocktail full of plenty of jalapeño heat.

GLASSWARE: Double rocks
GARNISH: Dehydrated slice of jalapeño

- Lava salt and cumin, to rim
- 1½ oz. Spicy Mezcal
- ¼ oz. Giffard Banane du Brésil Liqueur
- ½ oz. fresh lime juice
- ½ oz. Manzanilla sherry
- ¾ oz. tamarind syrup

1. Rim the double rocks glass with lava salt and cumin.

2. Combine all of the ingredients in a cocktail shaker with ice, shake vigorously, and strain into the glass over ice.

3. Garnish with dehydrated slice of jalapeño

SPICY MEZCAL: Add sliced jalapeño to a bottle of mezcal and let stand for at least 24 hours—determine the amount of jalapeños and the length of time you infuse mezcal based on your spice tolerance. Strain and store. Besharam uses the leftover jalapeños to garnish Bloody Marys, or as a boozy and yummy snack.

· MEZCAL ALOE MODE ·

THE SEA STAR

This Dogpatch neighborhood bar can be many different things to many kinds of patrons. It is the local pub for taking shots and playing pool. It has a strong craft beer roster. And, most of all, it has excellent cocktail creations from owner Alicia Walton. I happen to go to The Sea Star relatively frequently, sometimes when I want a great nearby cocktail, other times when I need to watch an important sporting event, or I happen to have a free hour and have a hankering for a terrific hazy IPA—or all three at once. It's such a fun place.

This cocktail by Walton will win over all the mezcal fans and mezcal skeptics in the room. It also has one of the greatest cocktail names ever, which really counts for something since creating a name can be the hardest part of making a drink.

GLASSWARE: Double rocks glass
GARNISH: Dehydrated lime wheel and black sea salt

- 2 oz. Del Maguey Vida Mezcal
- ¾ oz. Chareau Aloe Liqueur
- ¼ oz. agave syrup
- 3 dashes Bitter Queens 5 Spice Bitters
- 6 drops apple cider vinegar

1. Combine all of the ingredients in a mixing glass with ice, stir, and strain into the glass over a large ice cube.

2. Garnish with a dehydrated lime wheel and black sea salt.

· CARRIED AWAY ·

THE SEA STAR

Now for something entirely different than anything else in this book. Alicia Walton brings together two totally different worlds (aquavit and coconut) into one crisply constructed cocktail. It's easy to get carried away ordering a second round.

GLASSWARE: Snifter

GARNISH: Lime wheels and grated cinnamon

- 1½ oz. Krogstad Aquavit
- ¾ oz. Clement Mahina Coconut Liqueur
- ½ oz. fresh lemon juice
- ¼ oz. honey syrup

1. Combine all of the ingredients in a cocktail shaker with medium ice, shake vigorously, and strain into a snifter over ice.

2. Garnish with 3 quarter lime wheels and freshly grated cinnamon.

Van Ness Ave., California
59
& Market   Streets

DOWNTOWN, SOMA

Van Ness Ave., California
50
& Market Streets

& DES!GN DISTR!CT

ANANDA SPRITZ

FARM & VINE

THE LAST PHARAOH

GIN + TONIC

MI AMIGO

LAVENDER DREAMS

THE ROBIN'S NEST

ISLAND HOPPER

BROOKLYN HOLIDAY

E. HONDA

VEGA

SIMPLY RED

With so many banks and investment companies residing in our skyscrapers, it's easy to consider San Francisco's Financial District the "Wall Street of the West." Just hang out at happy hour in a popular bar or watch the sea of commuters walking from offices to BART stations and you'll see what I mean. SoMa refers to South of Market Street, our most important commercial street. It's a broad neighborhood that realistically is many neighborhoods, and includes landmarks like Oracle Park, SF MoMA, and the Moscone Center. SoMa is where the Bay Bridge starts/ends on the San Francisco side and also has the greatest concentration of start-up companies in the city. Much of the neighborhood used to be warehouses and garages. Those spaces are now the home of many of those start-ups, plus nightclubs, restaurants, and bars. It is San Francisco's chameleon neighborhood. Ask a hundred people what constitutes SoMa and you'll get a hundred different answers.

· ANANDA SPRITZ ·

BURMA CLUB

The Outer Richmond's Burma Superstar has been a San Francisco dining staple since the early 1990s. As Bay Area crowds are just as hungry for the tea leaf salad as they've ever been, the original restaurant has slowly morphed into a San Francisco- and East Bay-based group with a few different concepts. Their three-story SoMa restaurant, Burma Club, is certainly the glitziest of the Burma Inc roster and features notable cocktails, like this intriguing spritz of pineapple, bourbon, amaro, and bubbles—a long way from a regular ol' bourbon and sparkling wine Seelbach.

GLASSWARE: Cocktail glass
GARNISH: Edible flowers

- 5 pineapple chunks
- 1½ oz. Knob Creek Bourbon
- 1 oz. Amaro Nonino
- 3 dashes Angostura Bitters
- ½ oz. palm sugar syrup
- ½ oz. fresh lemon juice
- ½ oz. pineapple juice
- ¾ oz. sparkling wine

1. Muddle the pineapple in a cocktail shaker and then add all of the remaining ingredients, except the sparkling wine, and ice and shake vigorously.

2. Strain into a cocktail glass, top with sparkling wine, and garnish with edible flowers.

NIKU STEAKHOUSE

Outside of martinis at Harris' and The House of Prime Rib, San Francisco isn't really a steakhouse-and-cocktails kind of town. Remember, *nothing* pairs better with some red meat than a bold Napa cabernet sauvignon (if your wallet is feeling heavy). Our city's newest and splashiest steakhouse, Niku Steakhouse, focuses on Wagyu cuts, which obviously go well with red wine or martinis, but also pair nicely with some of the city's most innovative cocktails. Heck, you could be a vegetarian and have a great time with the food and cocktails at this Design District restaurant. It's an excellent concept from the Omakase Group, one of the city's most important power restaurant groups at the moment.

According to bar manager Ilya Romanov, "This unique cocktail features a pantry full of ingredients that you typically find dusting up at a bar and rarely find a use for." He uses an aquavit produced in New York as the base.

And, as a side note, San Francisco bartenders seem to love sugar snap peas. When it's springtime, they are on nearly every craft cocktail bar menu.

GLASSWARE: Old Fashioned glass
GARNISH: Shiso leaf and Umeboshi Powder

- 1 oz. Svol Swedish-Style Aquavit
- ¾ oz. La Gitana Manzanilla Sherry
- ½ oz. Napa Valley Fusion Verjus Blanc
- ¾ oz. fresh lime juice
- ¾ oz. Sugar Snap Pea Syrup
- ½ oz. egg white
- 1 oz. Q Mixers Elderflower Tonic

1. Combine all of the ingredients, except the elderflower tonic, in a cocktail shaker and shake without ice for 10 seconds. Add ice and hard-shake for an additional 10 seconds.

2. Add the elderflower tonic to the tin and strain contents into a glass. Add a couple of ice cubes to keep the cocktail cold.

3. Garnish with shies leaf and Umeboshi Powder.

SUGAR SNAP PEA SYRUP: Wash and juice 2 lbs. sugar snap peas to yield 5⅓ oz. snap pea juice. Add 4 oz. water to a saucepan and bring to a boil. When the water boils, add 16 oz. cane sugar and whisk until the sugar is fully diluted. Remove the pan from heat and let cool. Add the snap pea juice to the syrup and stir until fully incorporated. Bottle and use within 3 days.

UMEBOSHI POWDER: Using a dehydrator on a setting for vegetables, spread out pitted and pickled umeboshi plums on a tray and dehydrate for 3 days. This will produce a perfectly dry plum, which can be ground into a powder and used to, in the words of Ilya Romanov, "add a salty-savory-funk note."

MICHAEL MINA

Here's a glamorous showcase for Jean-Charles Boisset's French caviar-infused vodka, made from chardonnay grapes in Burgundy. Try it on its own, then enjoy this exquisite creation by one of San Francisco's most visionary bar talents, Anthony Attanasio of Michael Mina's downtown flagship restaurant. The Ana spice blend is based off of the house spice blend offered in the restaurant.

GLASSWARE: Tall coupe
GARNISH: Lime peel and basil leaf

- 1 oz. JCB Caviar Vodka
- ½ oz. Tanqueray Gin
- ½ oz. Yellow Chartreuse
- ½ oz. Ana Spice Syrup
- ½ oz. fresh lime juice

1. Combine all of the ingredients in a cocktail shaker with ice, shake vigorously, and double strain into the coupe.

2. Garnish with a lime peel and basil leaf.

ANA SPICE SYRUP: Combine 1 cup sugar and 1 cup water in a saucepan and bring to a boil. Remove the pan from heat and add 10 basil leaves and ¼ cup spice blend (equal amount of sesame, rose petal, sumac; all dried). Cover and let steep for 15 minutes. After 15 minutes, chill using an ice bath, strain, and store.

· GIN + TONIC ·

BELLOTA

San Francisco summers can feel like winter . . . and our winters can sometimes feel like summer. That means it's always gin and tonic season here! The Absinthe Group's spectacular Spanish restaurant in the Design District (it's located inside Airbnb's headquarters) is the city's best place for a mini Barcelona-evoking staycation with tapas, paellas, sherry, and plenty of Gin + Tonic.

GLASSWARE: Copa de Ballon, or any red wine glass
GARNISH: Lemon and lime wheels, sprigs of rosemary and thyme, manzanilla olive, and dried juniper berries

• 2 oz. Gin Mare

• Fever-Tree Mediterranean Tonic, to taste

1. Add gin to the glass over ice.

2. Pour tonic to taste (usually a fair amount since it's meant to be a re-freshing drink, but whatever you choose surely is right).

3. Garnish with lemon and lime wheels, sprigs of rosemary and thyme, manzanilla olive, and dried juniper berries.

JONNY RAGLIN
THE ABSINTHE GROUP

Enough of me telling you about San Francisco's modern cocktail history—it's time to hear from one of the key figures who was a pivotal part of that story. Jonny Raglin, now the Absinthe Group's director of bars and development, was one of the bartenders at Absinthe Brasserie & Bar who was making this history happen in San Francisco in the late 1990s. He was at the place at the moment when cocktail tastes started shifting toward the exciting world it is today. Let's allow him to tell you his firsthand experience.

HOW DID YOU GET YOUR START IN COCKTAILS AND BECOME INTERESTED IN CRAFT COCKTAILS, BEFORE CRAFT COCKTAILS WAS EVEN A THING?
My first restaurant job was a quasi-fancy Cajun spot in Oklahoma City with a recognizable bar culture. All the cool people hung out at the bar there and the bartenders were like local celebrities. I knew once I turned 21, I wanted to be a bartender. I befriended the bartenders, who to this day are some of my best friends, and they taught me everything they knew about cocktails which, in 1996 was pretty limited. Even though fresh juices and obscure historical cocktails were not a thing back then, we took pride in making drinks as delicious as possible and learning as much as we could about the history of cocktails and bars. This was the birth of the "craft cocktail" movement. A few years later I moved to San Francisco to pursue a career in bartending. I didn't really know what I was going to do with my life at the time, but in retrospect, I knew I could tend bar better than most and make a decent living at it. I just didn't know how big of a "thing" cocktail bartending would become. As an eager bartender in 2000 in San Francisco, I was in the right place at the right time.

MANY BARTENDERS THAT I'VE SPOKEN TO SAY THAT ABSINTHE WAS THE PLACE IN SAN FRANCISCO THAT STARTED THE WHOLE ELEVATED COCKTAIL MOVEMENT IN THE 90S. WOULD YOU AGREE?

There are multiple places that elevated the cocktail movement in San Francisco, but very few of those are still around. My first job in the city was at Stars. It opened in 1984 and the chef, Jeremiah Tower, was arguably the first "celebrity chef" in the country. The bar there was something like 80 feet long and cocktails were king. It was the first bar that I worked at that was completely fresh juice, which was kind of the litmus test for if a bar was really craft or not. Marco Dionysos was a bartender at Stars, and he left in the late 90s to open Absinthe. Stars closed in 2003, and when it did, Absinthe became the sole destination in the neighborhood for classic and craft cocktails.

CAN YOU TELL US A LITTLE ABOUT THAT ALL-STAR TEAM AT ABSINTHE WITH MARCO, YOU AND YOUR COLLEAGUES?

Marco really set the bar high in 1998. His opening menu was the biggest game changer in the scene. You couldn't find a sazerac in New York or New Orleans in 1998, but there was one on the opening menu at Absinthe. His signature house cocktail, the Ginger Rogers, is still one of the most popular drinks we serve. If you worked a cool bar twenty years ago, everyone was drinking mojitos, and while you could get a great one at Absinthe, the Ginger Rogers was the variation that became a hit. It was like a miracle in those days to get someone to even try gin, but once they got their lips on a Ginger Rogers, they were hooked.

OUTSIDE OF ABSINTHE, WHO WERE SOME OF THE OTHER MAJOR GAME-CHANGERS IN THE LOCAL MODERN COCKTAIL MOVEMENT?

Like I was saying about mojitos, they were a sign of a bartender that cared about the craft. Nobody made them more than David Nepove at Enrico's. He was a towering figure behind the bar, his smile was contagious, and the place was like a Latin heaven on Earth. My memories of having mojitos there were pivotal to my growth as a bartender. The cocktails had to be delicious, but the score conducted by the bartender had to be pitch-perfect. The mojito is still one of my top three cocktails of all time.

HOW HAS CREATING COCKTAILS CHANGED IN THE TIME SINCE ABSINTHE OPENED? DIFFERENT TECHNIQUES, PREFERENCES, INGREDIENTS?

Frankly, I don't think the results of cocktail creation are much different considering how different the approach is nowadays. The glaring difference between twenty years ago and now is our access to information. We really used to ply our craft in our own personal bubbles. We scoured used book stores for old cocktail books and hoped someone (anyone) would write something new that wasn't the typical "How to bartend" bullshit. That day finally came when Gary Regan released his book, The *Joy of Mixology*. His book really galvanized the burgeoning cocktail movement all over the country, but especially here in San Francisco because Gary wrote the regular *San Francisco Chronicle* column called "The Cocktailian." Gary Regan was like a godfather to so many bartenders back then. When he featured one of my cocktails in 2005, I became an overnight sensation. It was like everyone knew me or wanted to—it was totally crazy. Now, virtually any information you need about cocktail ingredients, recipes, history, etc. is just a Google search away. I think that proximity to information has diluted the cocktail scene and the craft to a certain degree as well. I often say that bars are best when they ply their trade in folklore, not facts. Now that every patron has the facts on their phone, there is little room for even accidental variation. This has created a more homogenized bar environment where people's expectations are sometimes higher than can be expected, and that has changed how we tend bar. Our focus is much less on the products we serve and how we mix and create cocktails and much more on the elements of excellent service. Most people would prefer a friendly bartender that runs their bar like a festive community gathering even if the cocktail isn't top-notch. We just strive to do both.

ANY FAVORITE BAY AREA COCKTAIL STORIES FROM YOUR UNIQUE PERSPECTIVE BEHIND THE BAR?

Back in 2001, I was the daytime bartender at Stars. The post-9/11 city was kind of a ghost town and my bar was pretty empty most days, so cranking out cocktails was no longer the focus. In between making fresh juice for the night bartenders, I might get the opportunity to test out the skills I was developing. An older gentleman came in one afternoon, put his Leica Rangefinder camera on the bar, and asked me how my margaritas were. Without batting an eye, I told him I made the best one in the world. I'm sure he figured I was just an upstart bartender, but I knew I made a damn good one. I had just taken an interest in photography, so I complimented him on his camera. He went on to tell me he had been taking pictures with that camera for the past 40 years. He was pretty friendly for an old guy, so I asked him a few things about taking pictures and he asked me a few things about the bottles behind me. As he got up to leave, I asked him how his margarita was. "Best in the world, right?" he said as he walked away. He came back every month or so in the afternoons and would have a margarita. We came to know each other by name. Jim never got very detailed with his stories, and when I would ask him about different subject matter for photos, he kept things very vague. I really wanted to know his story because he had such a fascinating disposition. So, like any good detective would, I took note of his last name on his credit card and decided to do a Nexus search on the computer when I got home. It turned out that Jim Marshall was one of the most accomplished photographers in the 20th century, taking the most intimate photos of rock 'n' roll icons, movie stars, and more. I couldn't fucking believe it. Jim would come in to visit after that and we would do our usual routine. It was so hard for me not to let on about what I had learned about him—he was like a hero to me. Still, I knew that the relationship I had with Jim had nothing to do with who he was or what he had done in his life. He was just a guy at a bar who liked my margaritas, and I think that's exactly how he liked it. So that is how it stayed until that bar closed. Some years later I saw Jim at the Washbag in North Beach. I came up, said hi, and he looked at me and said "Best margarita in the world?" Greatest honor of my bartending career.

· MI AMIGO ·

THE BRIXTON ON 2ND

It's hard to miss this cinnamon and spice-driven tequila sour (just look for the "B" stenciled garnish) at the SoMa sibling to the original Brixton on Union Street in Cow Hollow. The cocktail options are extensive at The Brixton, but I'll steer you to their strong roster of agave spirit cocktails (and agave spirits neat). In addition, by virtue of being one block from Oracle Park, it's a fantastic stop for a beer before the game and/or a Mi Amigo afterward to celebrate a Giants win.

GLASSWARE: Coupe

- 1 egg white
- 1½ oz. Casamigos Reposado Tequila
- 1 oz. fresh lime juice
- 1 oz. Cinnamon-Infused Agave
- 3 dashes Firewater Bitters
- Peychaud's Bitters, for stenciling

1. Dry shake the egg white in a cocktail shaker. Add the rest of the ingredients and shake with ice. Double strain.

2. Use an atomizer to spray Peychaud's Bitters over a "B" stencil (or any creative stencil or just add a few dots of the bitters with an atomizer).

CINNAMON-INFUSED AGAVE: Add 2 cinnamon sticks to 1 cup agave nectar and 1 cup water in a saucepan over medium heat and simmer for 10 to 15 minutes, stirring frequently. Let cool, strain, and store.

· LAVENDER DREAMS ·

LOCH & UNION DISTILLING

The excellent dry gin from the young Napa distillery is the base of this elegant cocktail by Anthony Attanasio, the lead bartender of FiDi power restaurant Michael Mina, the flagship of the eponymous chef's extensive global restaurant group. Sure, the gin would make a stellar martini or Negroni, but it is also a fantastic companion for strawberry and lavender bubbles! Yes, lavender bubbles. What are those? I'll let Mr. Attanasio explain below. Spoiler alert: it has nothing to do with Champagne.

GLASSWARE: Coupe

- ½ oz. Loch & Union American Dry Gin
- ½ oz. Giffard Wild Elderflower Liqueur
- ½ oz. Strawberry Syrup
- ½ oz. fresh lemon juice
- Lavender Bubbles

1. Combine all of the ingredients, except the Lavender Bubbles, in a cocktail shaker with ice, shake vigorously, and double strain into the glass.

2. Spoon bubbles on top.

STRAWBERRY SYRUP: Add 1½ cups chopped strawberries to a saucepan over low heat and cook until soft. Muddle the cooked strawberries in the pan and then add 1 cup sugar and 1 cup water and bring to a boil. Remove the pan from the heat and cover for 15 minutes. After 15 minutes, use an ice bath to chill the mixture, then strain and store.

LAVENDER BUBBLES: In a saucepan, combine 5 tablespoons sugar with 1 cup water and 5 grams dried lavender. Bring to a boil, remove from heat, and cover for 15 minutes. Chill using an ice bath, strain, and then weigh out 400 grams of liquid and add to it 2 grams of xanthan gum and 2.5 grams of Versawhip. Use a hand blender to incorporate. Use a handheld milk frother to create the bubbles.

· THE ROBIN'S NEST ·

TRAILBLAZER TAVERN

Michael Mina's partnership with two of Honolulu's top chefs, wife-and-husband team Michelle Karr-Ueoka and Wade Ueoka, provides a definitive Hawaiian regional cuisine dining experience 3,000 miles away from the Islands . . .in one of Downtown San Francisco's giant Salesforce office buildings (not the famous tall one). Sure, it isn't 80 degrees with trade winds outside like on Oahu, but the S.P.A.M. Musubi (mochi-crusted smoked pork arabiki meatloaf as a sushi-like roll) and drinks like Ryan Twedt's The Robin's Nest at least provide a brief vacation.

GLASSWARE: Hurricane glass
GARNISH: Candied pineapple wedge, a maraschino cherry on a bamboo skewer, and an umbrella pick

- 1 oz. Suntory Toki Japanese Whisky
- ½ oz. Plantation O.F.T.D. (or similar blended overproof rum)
- ½ oz. TBT Cinnamon Syrup
- ½ oz. fresh lemon juice
- ¾ oz. pineapple juice
- 1 oz. TBT Passion Honey Syrup
- 1 oz. cranberry juice

1. Combine all of the ingredients, except the cranberry juice, in a cocktail shaker with ice, shake vigorously, and strain into a hurricane glass.

2. Fill with crushed ice, top with cranberry juice float, and garnish with candied pineapple wedge and maraschino cherry on a bamboo skewer.

TBT CINNAMON SYRUP: In a saucepan, bring a 1:1 simple syrup to a simmer. Add 8 to 12 whole cinnamon sticks per gallon of syrup, remove the pan from the heat, and steep for a few hours. Strain and store.

TBT PASSION HONEY SYRUP: In a bowl, combine 2 parts passion fruit puree with 1 part honey and mix well.

· ISLAND HOPPER ·

TRAILBLAZER TAVERN

Freshly-pressed Hawaiian sugarcane produces some fantastic rum, and fortunately, there is a small crop of young, exciting distilleries that have recently opened up in the Islands. Many San Franciscans are learning during their Hawaiian vacations how great these rum producers like Koloa Rum Company (Kauai) and KoHana Distillers (Oahu) really are, and hope that we can see more bars use them in cocktails (or poured neat) back home. Ryan Twedt's invention here nicely lends itself to a perfect beach drink and a complex cocktail for rum geeks.

GLASSWARE: Collins glass
GARNISH: Pineapple fronds and dehydrated lime wheel

- 1 oz. Don Q Cristal Rum
- ½ oz. KoHana Kea Agricole
- ½ oz. TBT Hibiscus Syrup
- ½ oz. fresh lemon juice
- ¾ oz. pineapple juice
- 2 oz. ginger beer

1. Combine all of the ingredients, except the ginger beer, in a cocktail shaker and shake vigorously

2. Add the ginger beer to a Collins glass, then single strain the shaker's ingredients into the Collins glass.

3. Fill with crushed ice and garnish with pineapple fronds and a dehydrated lime wheel.

TBT HIBISCUS SYRUP: In a large container, combine 2 cups dried hibiscus flowers with 1 gallon simple syrup, let stand for a few hours, then strain and store.

· BROOKLYN HOLIDAY ·

THE VAULT

Located at the bottom of the giant 555 California Street skyscraper, The Vault is easily the most ambitious, swankiest concept from the popular Hi Neighbor Group (and during the COVID-19 pandemic, The Vault Garden took over the skyscraper's ground-level plaza, transforming blank urban open space into the city's most spectacular outdoor dining setting). One of their highlight cocktails, devised by Tyler Groom, takes a cue from a classic Brooklyn, then indeed sends it on a European holiday for something truly smooth and unique.

GLASSWARE: Rocks glass

GARNISH: Orange peel

- 1½ oz. rye whiskey
- ¾ oz. sweet vermouth
- ½ oz. Aperol
- ½ oz. Lillet Blanc

1. Combine all of the ingredients in a mixing glass and stir.

2. Pour into rocks glass over ice and garnish with an orange peel.

· E. HONDA ·

PABU

Alright, Street Fighter video game fans, here's the cocktail for you. Lead bartender Raymundo "Mundo" Delgado created this rich, umami-filled egg white cocktail as part of the Street Fighter-themed menu for the Financial District's bustling Japanese restaurant from chefs Ken Tominaga and Michael Mina. Mundo creates some of the most creative menus in all of San Francisco, both visually and in terms of the intriguing drinks themselves.

GLASSWARE: Ceramic mug

- 2 oz. Wagyu Fat-Washed Suntory Toki Japanese Whisky
- ¾ oz. fresh lemon juice
- ½ oz. Togarashi Syrup
- ½ oz. egg whites
- 1 dash Peychaud's Bitters

1. Combine all of the ingredients in a cocktail shaker with ice, shake vigorously, and strain into a ceramic mug.

WAGYU FAT-WASHED SUNTORY TOKI JAPANESE WHISKY: Pour 1 (700 ml) bottle of Suntory Toki Whisky into a cambrio. In a small pan, cook 3 oz. Wagyu steak; when done, combine rendered fat with the whisky. Refrigerate overnight, strain, and store.

TOGARASHI SYRUP: In a small saucepan, combine 20 oz. agave syrup and 20 oz. water and bring to a simmer; slowly add 100 ml togarashi and mix well. Let cool, strain, and store.

· VEGA ·

PABU

Raymond Delgado's Vega is on the lighter, more elegant side of the cocktail spectrum compared to the E. Honda (no Wagyu fat here). The nutty, deeply savory Manzanilla and Japanese whisky tandem is gently tied together by some papaya shrub and Cardamaro (an apéritif). It's the perfect companion for pork gyoza and sushi to start at Pabu, before later partnering sake with robata-grilled items and miso-marinated black cod.

GLASSWARE: Tall glass

- 1½ oz. Lustau Manzanilla Sherry
- ½ oz. White Oak Akashi Japanese Whisky
- ½ oz. papaya shrub
- ½ oz. Cardamaro
- 2 dashes Degroff's Pimento Bitters

1. Combine all of the ingredients in a cocktail shaker and shake. Strain over ice into a tall glass.

· SIMPLY RED ·

This bar and the Virgin Hotel where it was located have closed, but that's no reason not to celebrate Megan Abraham's always compelling cocktails, balancing the thoughtful line of being unique yet never overly complex. Doubtless the reason she landed the job as creative beverage director for Mourad and Aziza.

GLASSWARE: Coupe
GARNISH: Dill sprig and dusted cinnamon

- 2 oz. Zephyr Gin
- 1 oz. Simply Red Syrup
- ½ oz. fresh lime juice
- ¾ oz. egg whites
- 3 dashes Old-Fashioned bitters

1. Combine all of the ingredients in a cocktail shaker and dry shake. Add ice, shake until chilled, and double strain.

2. Garnish with the dill sprig and dusted cinnamon.

SIMPLY RED SYRUP: Combine equal parts Dill Simple Syrup and pomegranate puree or pomegranate juice. Let steep with sumac and Urfa biber for 15 minutes. Strain and store.

DILL SIMPLE SYRUP: Boil 2 cups water, remove from heat, add 5 sprigs dill, and steep for 4 minutes. Strain and stir in 2 cups sugar, mixing until all the sugar dissolves.

· WH!STLE PODU ·

ROOH

With locations in SoMa and Palo Alto, ROOH is one of the Bay Area's defining contemporary Indian restaurants. There are all sorts of tech-advanced, modern techniques involved in the cocktails and food (like carbonation for this cocktail), but it's always to enhance the core purpose of each dish and drink. It isn't glitzy just to be glitzy. Here's head mixologist Chetan Gangan to describe a not-so-typical Bloody Mary: "'Whistlepodu' means "to cheer" by blowing a whistle. It's our take on a Bloody Mary, with traditional rasam, which is a spicy and sour tomato soup from Southern India."

GLASSWARE: Rocks glass
GARNISH: Fried curry leaf

- 2 oz. Smoked Rasam
- 2 oz. vodka
- ¾ oz. honey
- ¾ oz. fresh lime juice
- 1 oz. soda

1. Combine all of the ingredients in a mixing glass, stir, and then carbonate (ROOH uses a Fizzini soda maker).

2. Serve in a rocks glass over ice and garnish with fried curry leaf.

SMOKED RASAM: Dice 15 tomatoes, place them in a saucepan over medium heat, and cook for about 20 minutes. Add coriander and curry leaves, mustard seeds, and ROOH Masala Water to the tomatoes, stir to combine and then smoke for 1 hour.

NORTH BEACH /

CHINATOWN / EMBARCADERO

HOG ISLAND BLOODY MARY

OYSTER MARTINI VESPER

SEA COLLINS

TEQUILA MOCKINGBIRD

WHISKEY VIC

HANGTOWN DRY

SOMETIMES OLD FASHIONED

THE COUNTRY LAWYER

NOISY BOY

ROSA

PIMM'S CUP

15 ROMOLO ESPRESSO MARTINI

North Beach (our "Little Italy") and Chinatown are San Francisco's key historical neighborhoods. Chinatown is the largest outside of Asia and centers on Grant Avenue. Next door is North Beach, which indeed used to be the waterfront before the landfill pushed the Bay east (spoiler alert: there is no North Beach *beach*). North Beach is the intellectual, Bohemian center of San Francisco, where the Beat Generation hung out and where literary fans still linger for hours in City Lights Bookstore. There are several old-school Italian family businesses and restaurants in North Beach, though, sadly, those seem to be dwindling each year. The Embarcadero is the spectacular palm tree-lined waterfront road full of happy joggers and walkers, plus ferry commuters arriving at the majestic Ferry Building. It wasn't that long ago, however, when this was an ugly elevated freeway, only to be demolished after the 1989 earthquake. Luckily, you can barely imagine that today when savoring the panoramic views.

· HOG ISLAND BLOODY MARY ·

HOG ISLAND OYSTER CO.

There are few pleasures in San Francisco that are more enjoyable than gazing out at the Bay with a dozen oysters and a sharp libation at Hog Island Oyster Company's Ferry Building location. It's a bit of a hike (and a challenge to get a reservation) to go to Hog Island's oyster habitat home in Marshall on west Marin County's Tomales Bay, plus there isn't a full bar. For the perfect oysters and cocktails pairing, it must be the Ferry Building, which is hardly a letdown (or the newly opened location in Larkspur). When it's brunch time, I'll skip mimosas with the oysters in favor of a Bloody Mary that will power anyone through any Sunday morning fatigue. And, yes, the recipe is built for four (though I'm not judging if there is a party of one), and indeed there is Hog's Blood and Hogwash involved, but neither involves pigs.

GLASSWARE: Collins glass
GARNISH: Pickled vegetables or Castelvetrano olives

- 6 oz. vodka
- 12 oz. tomato juice
- 1 oz. seasoned rice vinegar
- 1 oz. unseasoned rice vinegar
- 1 oz. Worcestershire sauce
- 1 oz. fresh lemon juice
- 1 oz. extra hot horseradish

- 16 dashes Tapatio or Crystal Hot Sauce
- 8 dashes celery bitters
- 4 pinches salt
- 20 cracks of pepper
- 1 bar spoon Hogwash Mignonette, per drink

1. Add all of the ingredients, except the mignonette, to a serving pitcher and whisk to combine.

2. Fill glasses with ice and pour equal amounts of the mixture (aka Hogs Blood) into 4 glasses.

3. Garnish with pickled vegetables or Castelvetrano olives and top each drink with 1 bar spoon of Hogwash Mignonette.

HOGWASH MIGNONETTE: In a bowl, combine 1 large shallot, peeled and minced, 1 large jalapeño, seeded and minced, and ½ bunch cilantro, finely chopped, and mix well. Just before serving, add juice of 1 lime, ¼ cup seasoned rice vinegar, and ¼ cup unseasoned rice vinegar to the mixture. Use the same day it's made.

· OYSTER MARTINI VESPER ·

HOG ISLAND OYSTER CO.

Sure, a crisp Sancerre or Muscadet is technically the ideal pairing for oysters, or so say all those formal sommelier training books. Trust me, *the* ideal pairing is an ice-cold martini or vesper, especially one that involves an Oakland-produced oyster gin and a tincture with subtle mignonette notes.

GLASSWARE: Coupe
GARNISH: Lemon twist and Sweetwater oyster on the half shell

- 3 oz. Oakland Spirits Co. Halfshell Oyster Gin
- ¼ oz. Oyster Vesper Blend

1. Combine the ingredients in a mixing glass with ice, stir until chilled, and strain into a coupe.

2. Garnish with a lemon twist and a Sweetwater oyster served on the half shell.

OYSTER VESPER BLEND: Combine equal parts Lillet Blanc, Dolin Dry Vermouth, Tempus Fugit Kina L'Aéro d'Or Apéritif, and Black Peppercorn Lemon Tincture and mix well.

BLACK PEPPERCORN LEMON TINCTURE: Fill a mason jar half full with black peppercorns. Fill the rest of the jar with lemon peels. Add high-proof neutral grain alcohol or grape distillate until liquid covers the lemon peels. Cover and let sit at room temperature for 2 weeks. Strain and store.

· SEA COLLINS ·

HOG ISLAND OYSTER CO.

The good folks at Oakland Spirits Company certainly have fun with their gin. The aforementioned Halfshell Gin is a London Dry style, for which 200 Hog Island Sweetwater oysters are crushed in the distilling process. For this version of a Tom Collins which is vividly inspired by the seaweed- and kelp-filled Northern California coast, the Oakland Spirits Company Sea Gin is the drink's briny anchor, packed with foraged nori, lemongrass, and some other elements of our coastal terroir.

GLASSWARE: Collins glass
GARNISH: 2 or 3 nori leaves

- 2 oz. Oakland Spirits Company Automatic Sea Gin
- ¾ oz. Seaweed-Infused Honey
- ½ oz. fresh lemon juice
- ½ oz. fresh lime juice
- 4 dashes chamomile tincture
- Soda water, to top

1. Combine all of the ingredients, except soda water, in a cocktail shaker with a medium amount of ice, shake vigorously, and double strain into a Collins glass.

2. Top with soda water and lightly stir with a bar spoon.

3. Garnish with nori leaves, gently stirring the seaweed into the cocktail to create the appearance of tidal water.

SEAWEED-INFUSED HONEY:
In a bowl, combine equal parts raw honey and water and mix well. Add dry nori seaweed and let sit at room temperature for 7 days. Strain, making sure to extract all liquid/flavor from seaweed, and store. (Hog Island uses 1½ cups seaweed per 1 liter of honey water)

TEQUILA MOCKINGBIRD

Get it? Yup, we thought so. As Gregory Peck comes to mind, try out this perfect post-work thirst quencher or summer refresher that is the namesake drink of Eric Passetti and Dennis Leary's relaxed SoMa bar. It's a particular 5:00 p.m. favorite for the neighborhood's young tech workers.

GLASSWARE: Tall glass

GARNISH: Grapefruit peel

- 2 oz. blanco tequila
- 1 oz. fresh lime juice
- ¾ oz. curaçao
- ¾ oz. elderflower liqueur
- ½ oz. grapefruit juice
- 2 dashes Angostura Bitters

1. Combine all of the ingredients in a cocktail shaker with ice, shake vigorously, and pour into a tall glass.

2. Garnish with the grapefruit peel.

NATOMA CABANA

On a SoMa alley by the massive (and massively delayed) Salesforce Transit Center, Natoma Cabana is probably the hippest of the Dennis Leary and Eric Passetti bars. It's a bustling happy hour spot earlier in the night, then charming and low-key with twinkling lights overhead later on. At any time, try this white whiskey (moonshine) version of a mai tai. Yes, that it isn't a typo. It's a great Appalachian twist on a tiki classic.

GLASSWARE: Collins glass

GARNISH: Cherry, orange, and lemon wedges

- 1½ oz. White Lightnin'
- ½ oz. curaçao
- ½ oz. orgeat
- ½ oz. fresh lime juice
- ¼ oz. fresh lemon juice

1. Combine all of the ingredients in a cocktail shaker with ice, shake vigorously, and strain into a Collins glass.

2. Garnish with cherry and orange and lemon wedges.

· HANGTOWN DRY ·

TERMINUS

Located at the California Street cable car turnaround, Terminus sports a Parisian casual-polished aesthetic right in the heart of downtown San Francisco. This is the most intimate of the Dennis Leary and Eric Passetti bars, always spilling out to the sidewalk with off-work bankers at 5:00 PM. Like its peers (Tequila Mockingbird, Natoma Cabana, The House of Shields), Terminus has another no-nonsense menu, filled with simple but excellent cocktails. The Hangtown Dry is a boozy nod to the Hangtown Fry, San Francisco's famous oyster-and-bacon omelette that is best enjoyed a few blocks down California Street at Tadich Grill (the oldest continually run restaurant in California).

GLASSWARE: Champagne saucer
GARNISH: Cherry

- 1½ oz. dry vermouth
- ¾ oz. Kirschwasser
- ½ oz. Crème de Cassis

1. Combine all of the ingredients in a mixing glass with ice, stir, and strain into a Champagne saucer.

2. Garnish with a cherry.

· SOMETIMES OLD FASHIONED ·

COLD DRINKS

On busy Broadway, where Chinatown meets North Beach, China Live is one of the Bay Area's most ambitious, extensive food and drink complexes. It's a marketplace, an elaborate tasting menu restaurant, a cafe, a main "market restaurant," a hidden lounge, and more to come from chef/restaurateur George Chen. Cold Drinks is the signature cocktail bar, located on the second floor. It's as swanky and stylish as it gets in San Francisco, boasting a stunning Shanghai jazz era (bartenders with tuxedos!) meets contemporary luxury design and vibe. Cold Drinks is also San Francisco's signature scotch bar, so it's appropriate that our cocktail recipe from lead bartender Yong Zhu heavily emphasizes the medium-bodied, elegant single malt from Speyburn.

GLASSWARE: Rocks glass
GARNISH: Mint sprig and lemon twist

- 1 oz. Duck Fat-Washed Speyburn 10 Scotch
- 1 oz. George Dickle Rye
- ¼ oz. Black Pepper Syrup
- 1 dash Alley 86'd Candy Cap Bitters
- 2 dashes Angostura Bitters
- 2 dashes Scrappy Lemon Bitters

1. Combine all of the ingredients in a mixing glass, stir, and strain into rocks glass over ice.

2. Garnish with mint spring and lemon twist.

Duck Fat-Washed Speyburn 10 Scotch: In a large container, combine 900 ml duck fat with 6 bottles of Speyburn Scotch (or use that ratio). Leave the batch at room temperature for 2 hours, then place the batch in the freezer overnight. The next day, pour the scotch through a coffee filter-lined funnel paper to catch all the fat. Bottle and store.

Black Pepper Syrup: In a container, gently muddle 20 grams black peppercorns. Add 1 liter water and 1,250 grams sugar to the peppercorns, mix well, and refrigerate overnight. Strain and store.

· THE COUNTRY LAWYER ·

PARK TAVERN

There is no finer digestif cocktail in San Francisco than the Big Night Restaurant Group's classic bourbon-amaro-vermouth sipper, created by Casey Doolin way back in 2011. I probably have this cocktail more than any other in the city. And, there's absolutely no reason not to have it during dinner as well to accompany the group's beloved Marlowe Burger.

GLASSWARE: Cocktail glass
GARNISH: Orange peel

- 1½ oz. Four Roses Bourbon
- ½ oz. Zucca Amaro
- ½ oz. Dolin Blanc
- ¼ oz. Benedictine
- 1 dash chocolate bitters

1. Combine all of the ingredients in a mixing glass, stir, and strain into a cocktail glass.

2. Garnish with an orange peel.

TONY'S PIZZA NAPOLETANA

As you arrive at beautiful Washington Square Park in the heart of North Beach with Coit Tower looming nearby atop Telegraph Hill, there is always a line in one corner of the park. Yes, that's Tony Gemignani's pizza spot. The pizza is incredible, but why wait for a table when you can (usually) sit at the bar without a wait, watch the cocktails from bar manager Elmer Mejicanos and his staff get energetically shaken and stirred, and have that same world-famous pizza. It's a win-win situation. Mejicanos is one of those great barmen who makes a major impact on every menu he deals with, whether it's spicy tequila drinks with pizza or twists on eggnog for holiday pop-ups. The catch is that he seems to have five projects happening at the same time usually, so it's hard to find him. At least now I know that he'll often be at Tony's, just like a few hundred pizza lovers each day.

GLASSWARE: Old Fashioned glass
GARNISH: Cucumber slice

- **2 oz. Serrano Pepper-Infused Blanco Tequila**
- **¾ oz. Agave Syrup**
- **1 oz. fresh lime juice**
- **1-inch slice of cucumber**

1. Combine all of the ingredients in a cocktail shaker and muddle the cucumber. Add ice, shake really hard for about 9 seconds, and strain into an Old Fashioned glass and top with ice.

2. Garnish with a cucumber slice.

SERRANO PEPPER-INFUSED TEQUILA: Add 1 sliced serrano pepper to a full bottle of blanco tequila. Let rest for 2 hours, strain, and return the tequila to the bottle.

AGAVE SYRUP: In a container, combine equal parts agave nectar and hot water and stir until completely mixed.

· ROSA ·

TONY'S PIZZA NAPOLETANA

Elmer Mejicanos partners tequila with two unusual teammates (Campari and Italian Bergamotto liqueur) in this tart and refreshing grapefruit drink. It's a very appealing aperitivo for guests looking for something in the fruity direction and something on the herbal amaro side of the spectrum.

GARNISH: Collins glass

GRAPEFRUIT: Grapefruit slice

- 1 oz. blanco tequila
- ½ oz. Campari
- ½ oz. Italicus Bergamotto Liqueur
- 2 oz. fresh grapefruit juice

1. Add all of the ingredients to a cocktail shaker with ice, shake really hard for about 9 seconds, and strain into a Collins glass.

2. Top with ice and garnish with a grapefruit slice.

· PIMM'S CUP ·

When Greg Lindgren and Jon Gasparini opened 15 Romolo on a tiny alley off the Broadway strip in North Beach in 1998, the same year that Absinthe Brasserie & Bar opened, nobody had any idea what the next twenty-two years would hold for cocktails. Both establishments just wanted to serve high-quality cocktails. Absinthe is more a restaurant with a bar while 15 Romolo is more of a bar with good food and the history of being in San Francisco's most historic cocktails neighborhood (it is attached to the Basque Hotel, which literally was a place for family-style Basque meals, and preceded by being brothels and speakeasies over the decades).

15 Romolo still has North Beach's fun, "l let the good times roll" edginess, but it is also very much a prime cocktail bar. It seems like nearly every major current local bartender has worked here.

Here's current bar manager David Vileta telling us about 15 Romolo's all-time best seller, the Pimm's Cup: "It has been on the menu for around ten years, right around when we remodeled and doubled down on the craft cocktail framework. Our Pimm's Cup was a front-runner for that concept. We deconstructed the classic and reworked it from a craft perspective, integrating fresh produce and eschewing commercial ginger beer in favor of house-made ingredients. We've also used the Pimm's as a wild card on our menu. Although traditionally a summer gin cocktail, its refreshing flavors have an affinity with virtually everything, everyone, and any occasion. So guests can and often do request alternative spirits. It's commonly ordered with vodka,

agave, or whiskey. We've even made Pimm's Cups with Fernet or absinthe, and the results always reward experimentation. Personally I like to split the gin with a rich, funky Jamaican rum."

GLASSWARE: Collins glass

GARNISH: Tuft of mint speared through a cucumber wheel

- 1 oz. gin
- 1 oz. Pimm's No.1
- 2 dashes Angostura Bitters
- ¾ oz. Ginger Syrup
- 3 slices cucumber
- 1 pinch mint
- 1 oz. fresh lemon juice
- 3-4 oz. seltzer water

1. Combine all of the ingredients, except seltzer water, in a cocktail shaker with ice, shake vigorously, and strain into a Collins glass.

2. Top with seltzer and ice to fill. Garnish with a tuft of mint speared through a cucumber wheel.

GINGER SYRUP: In a bowl, combine 3 parts fresh ginger juice to 1 part rich simple syrup (2:1 sugar to water), mix well, and store.

· 15 ROMOLO ESPRESSO MARTINI ·

While the Pimm's Cup goes back a decade, here's a previously too sweet/too rich/too everything dessert martini transformed into something thoughtful and well-composed that is a new favorite at 15 Romolo. The Irish Coffee has competition.

GLASSWARE: Cocktail glass
GARNISH: Black lava sea salt blended with coffee grounds

- 1 oz. vanilla bean vodka (15 Romolo uses Grey Goose La Vanille)
- 1 oz. cold brew coffee concentrate
- ¾ oz. Pedro Ximenez Sherry

1. Combine all of the ingredients in a cocktail shaker with ice, shake vigorously, and double strain quickly into the glass to retain as much frothy crema as possible.*

2. Garnish with a thin line of black lava sea salt blended with coffee grounds.

* *Note from David Vileta:* "It's very important with that shake to strain it off as soon as possible after the shake, otherwise the crema will stick to the ice in the tin, which can result in something that looks rather disappointing."

"A recent sensation—we sell nearly as many Espresso Martinis as Pimm's Cups. It's another familiar drink that was an easy target for reworking. Often these will have some combination of cream, coffee liqueur, maybe coffee itself on top of the liqueur. Recipes vary wildly from bar to bar.

"Our recipe is simple, elegant, and contemporary. There are only three very high-quality ingredients in the balance. We're always looking for ways to introduce the masses to sherry and its utility in cocktails, so our Espresso Martini has been the perfect vehicle for showing off Pedro Ximenez, the only source of sweetness here. It's crucial for weight and texture."—David Vileta

UNION SQUARE/NOB HILL/RUSSIAN HILL/

TENDERLOIN/HAYES VALLEY/CASTRO

LEEWARD NEGRONI

QUINCE

OLD-FASHIONED CURE ALL

KAGANO

RED TEMPLES

SLOE SUNSET

WITCH DOCTOR

THE LAST STRAWBERRY

SIMON SAYS

AIPUR EMERALD COCKTAIL

BOOTLEGGER'S BARREL DRINK

SAILOR'S GUILLOTINE

GREEN GOBLIN

CALIFORNIA COOLER

ZOMBIE KILLER

TOUSSAINT 91

PROPER CUP

THE SAN FRANCISCO TREAT

BOROUGH

ASYLUM HARBOR

These neighborhoods are the center of San Francisco. Union Square is the main shopping area and frequently where tourists stay when in the city. The neighboring Tenderloin is historically rich, and home to many important cocktail bars, but it's well-known that the neighborhood has not shaken off the challenges of its struggling street life. It's quite the juxtaposition to its neighbor up the big hill, Nob Hill, which is one of San Francisco's most stately neighborhoods. Russian Hill, home to curvy Lombard Street and the roller coaster portions of a cable car ride, is equally posh. Across Van Ness Avenue (our second "main street" after Market Street), Hayes Valley is an upscale boutiques-and-restaurants-filled area right by City Hall, the War Memorial Opera House, and Davies Symphony Hall. Just beyond Hayes Valley is the Castro, San Francisco's prominent gay neighborhood with decades of important history.

· LEEWARD NEGRONI ·

PACIFIC COCKTAIL HAVEN

San Francisco's most celebrated Negroni isn't exactly your normal gin-sweet vermouth-Campari creation. It isn't even a straight 1:1:1 ratio of the ingredients trio. Kevin Diedrich created this masterpiece for Negroni Week one year and it hasn't left the menu. The mixture of pandan and coconut with the botanicals of Sipsmith Very Junipery Over Proof Gin and Campari is nothing short of cocktail brilliance. I look forward to sipping one of these again soon at Pacific Cocktail Haven, once repairs from a devastating fire are completed.

GLASSWARE: Rocks glass

GARNISH: Pandan leaf

- **Bittermens Tiki Bitters, for rinsing**
- **1 oz. Coconut Oil Washed Campari**
- **¾ oz. Pandan Cordial**
- **½ oz. Sipsmith V.J.O.P.**

1. Rinse a rocks glass with the bitters then discard the bitters.

2. Combine all of the ingredients in a mixing glass with ice, stir, strain into the rocks glass over a single large ice cube, and garnish with pandan leaf.

COCONUT OIL WASHED CAMPARI: In a container with a lid, combine 16 oz. virgin coconut oil with 1 liter Campari and let sit, covered, at room temperature for 24 hours, stirring occasionally. After 24 hours, put the mixture into the freezer until the coconut oil fat freezes. Strain out the coconut oil fat through a coffee filter.

PANDAN CORDIAL: In a container with a lid, create Pandan Tincture by combining 10 pandan leaves cut into strips with 1 liter Everclear. Let sit at room temperature for 48 hours. Strain out leaves. Make Pandan Cordial by adding 12 oz. simple syrup to 8 oz. Pandan Tincture.

· QUINCE ·

THE STREAM OF CONSCIOUSNESS

Quince is not a cocktail bar. It's one of the most impressive Italian-influenced special occasion restaurants in the country, if not the world. And, as a tremendous bonus, the spirits, cocktails, and amaro program from the salon by the Pacific Avenue entrance is equally world-class. I wish you the best of luck trying to create an exact replica of this meticulous, captivating cocktail. However, with a little improvising, it *is* possible to make at home. A caramelized wood-influenced sugar without a barrel will be the primary challenging step at home. Or, if you ever have the chance and the means to do so, I can't recommend enough enjoying this cocktail at the restaurant, then spending three or four hours savoring the food of Chef Michael Tusk and his team:

I'll let Quince's Bar Chef Michael Kudra explain the cocktail: "The Stream of Consciousness is a cocktail based on wood molecules, combining different elements to expand the flavors of what happens when bourbon is resting in a barrel as it ages. First, I chose two different woods from the Bay Area that the Ohlone (the local Native American tribe) used for spicing, which was California Bay Laurel and Filbert (hazelnut). Fortunately, Quince has a wonderful farm in Bolinas (on the Marin County coast) and I was able to find these trees there. Once I had the wood, I replicated the process of making a bourbon barrel by drying out the wood for a number of months to amplify its flavor. I coated the wood with sugar and caramelized it with a blowtorch, creating a woodsy and velvet-textured syrup. The three other ingredients are maple syrup that has been rested in a bourbon barrel, a birch liquor from Iceland, and a 10 year-aged bourbon, Eagle Rare 10. The two other ingredients are my own bitters and winter citrus bitters that highlight the farmers markets, containing Buddha's hand, bearss lime (also known as Persian lime—not a typo), blood orange, Meyer lemon, lemon, pomelo, mandarins, Cara Cara oranges, and grapefruit.

It is meant to have similar texture and notes to an aged whiskey in a glass. [It is] named after William Faulkner's writing style, because he always had bourbon by his typewriter."

GLASSWARE: Japanese volcano glass
GARNISH: California bay leaf

- 2 oz. Eagle Rare 10 (or other fine bourbon)
- ½ oz. wood syrup
- ½ oz. Foss Birch Liqueur
- ½ oz. bourbon barrel maple syrup
- 6 dashes winter citrus bitters
- 4 dashes aromatic bitters
- 1 strip of orange peel, for expressing

1. Combine all of the ingredients, except the orange peel, in a mixing glass with ice and stir for thirty rotations.

2. Strain into Japanese volcano glass that is smoked with hazelnut wood.

3. Express orange peel over drink and discard. Garnish with the bay leaf.

· OLD-FASHIONED CURE ALL ·

RYE

15 Romolo's younger sibling (though older than almost any other craft cocktail bar in the city) continues to be a steadfast favorite at the edge of Lower Nob Hill and the Tenderloin. It's a more subdued hang out-type of place, best enjoyed with the signature Rock & Rye-based Old-Fashioned Cure All, which boasts an exciting depth and balance to please both fans of spirit-forward and less stiff drinks.

GLASSWARE: Old-Fashioned glass
GARNISH: Orange twist

- 2 oz. Rock & Rye
- ¼ oz. Tempus Fugit Crème de Cacao
- 3 dashes Angostura Bitters

1. Combine all of the ingredients in a mixing glass with ice, stir, and strain into the glass.

2. Garnish with the orange twist.

ROCK & RYE: In a container with a lid, combine 1 liter rye whiskey (100 proof and over), 3 cinnamon sticks, 8 Horehound rock candy pieces, 1 teaspoon cloves, and zests of 3 oranges and two lemons. Stir, cover, and let steep for two days. Strain and store.

JAMES GOAD

BALCONES DISTILLING

As a writer, you never know when you'll encounter an important source. While at an Off the Grid mobile food event at Fort Mason, I started talking with a bartender for Rye on the Road, the mobile off-shoot of Rye. As I kept talking with James Goad, I learned all about his extensive career at many of San Francisco's tentpole cocktail bars and restaurants. Goad now spends most of his time as the Northern California account manager for Balcones Distilling, but you should be able to reliably find him at some Rye on the Road events.

YOU'VE BEEN A PART OF THREE MAJOR SAN FRANCISCO RESTAURANTS—LOCANDA, SLOW CLUB, RED DOG—IN THREE NEIGHBORHOODS THAT HAVE GROWN RAPIDLY IN RECENT YEARS, IN LARGE PART BECAUSE OF THOSE RESTAURANTS. WHY DO YOU THINK THE RESTAURANTS MADE SUCH AN IMPACT IN THESE LOCATIONS?
In all three cases, there was a need to be filled in each neighborhood. Slow Club's neighborhood was primarily artists' studios and tech startup when they opened in the 90s—there was a need for a restaurant that could accommodate the lunch crowd while they became a dinner destination. The Mission wasn't filled with a glut of craft cocktail bars when Locanda opened, so they were the darling of that neighborhood in their first few years for sure. When I opened the first iteration of Red Dog there was a need for a large restaurant space with a craft bar program that could accommodate the tech crowd that populates 2nd Street.

HOW DO YOU SEE SLOW CLUB'S IMPACT ON THE LOCAL DINING AND COCKTAIL SCENE?
I think the Slow Club was instrumental in shaping the Mission food scene. They were one of the first restaurants to identify the impor-

tance of a farm-to-table approach. This philosophy carried over to the bar program—early menus featured classic cocktails and emphasized fresh local produce. When the craft cocktail movement came calling, we were quick to jump aboard and push the boundaries of creativity. I was lucky enough to manage their bar program for ten years.

WHAT HAVE YOU NOTICED ABOUT CHANGES IN CUSTOMERS AND THEIR TASTES BETWEEN STARTING AT SLOW CLUB AND NOW?

Customers' palates have definitely evolved and become more sophisticated. The "craft aesthetic" has spilled over into every aspect of consumer life, from coffee to bicycle shops. Customers these days are not only accepting of craft cocktails, they expect them. When I started featuring craft cocktails, raised my prices to reflect more expensive ingredients, and replaced fish bowl-sized martini glasses with delicate little coupes people lost their shit and there was talk of revolt. It now seems like so long ago.

FOR LOCANDA, CAN YOU TELL US A BIT ABOUT WORKING WITH AMAROS FOR COCKTAILS?

Working at Locanda and being exposed to a range of different amaros was definitely a game changer for me. They were a component or feature in everything I created there. They are delicious stand-alone drinks, as they are meant to be, but are also amazing sweetening and bittering agents in cocktails. There is so much range there, from bittersweet like Lucano or CioCiaro to Alpine spiced Braullio to bitter grippiness like Amaro Dell' Eroborista. And then there is a whole sub-category of Fernets to explore. Amaro Sibilia is still my favorite and there is always a bottle at home.

AND NOW YOU'RE AT RYE ON THE ROAD. HOW IS THAT TEAM ABLE TO MAKE LARGE BATCH COCKTAILS JUST AS SPECIAL AS AN INDIVIDUALLY MADE ONE YOU'D GET AT RYE OR ANOTHER INTIMATE, HIGH-QUALITY BAR?

They have a very talented commissary staff headed by Sarah Shaw, the former commissary manager of Future Bars. Whatever they can dream up, she can make a reality and streamline it to work in a large format. They've got it down to a science these days.

ANY FAVORITE COCKTAILS THAT YOU PERSONALLY LOVE TO MAKE?

I tend to like to drink and create spirit-forward drinks. I like Boulevardier and Old Fashioned riffs. I usually start with a shrub/syrup or liqueur and create a drink around them and then choose the base spirit. Sometimes, if the spirit is really unique and pronounced, I'll build components around it. In the case of the latter, I just put together an Old Fashioned riff using Balcones Brimstone Whisky—shameless plug!—coconut fat-washed-smoked-corn whisky, graham cracker syrup, and whisky barrel bitters.

WHAT ARE SOME OF THE KEY DIFFERENCES OF SWITCHING FROM NIGHTLY BARTENDER LIFE TO BEING AN ACCOUNT MANAGER?

Flexibility! My wife and I have a five-year-old. A fluid schedule is the key to our "success." The transition was definitely not seamless. There is a lot of admin and it's a constant work in progress to keep myself organized—but highly gratifying. I also have the privilege to work for a company that I've supported in the past as a buyer and believe in.

ANY FAVORITE STORIES FROM YOUR YEARS BEHIND THE BAR IN SAN FRANCISCO?

Perhaps not my proudest moment, or maybe it was. It happened while working my first bar gig in the late 90s. Murio's Trophy Room in Upper Haight, back in the days when all cocktail creation was in the form of a shot and tasted like it came out of a vending machine. A young woman asked me to make her a shot for her birthday. Back then I really liked lighting drinks on fire and this seemed fitting for a birthday request. I decided to join her. Put a little 151 on top to light it, I blew out the little blue flame, and down it went—but my new friend did not blow out her candle and proceeded to shoot it *en fuego*. She somehow ignited her nose with that little blue flame courtesy of the 151. I reacted swiftly and batted the flame out with an open hand. She was whisked away by her gal pals to the bathroom. She resurfaced, embarrassed, mascara-stained cheeks, little blisters on her nose, and very angry. She said, "Why didn't you tell me to blow it out?" to which I said, "Unless you're part of the circus, you don't drink fire!" As a follow-up, she returned a few months later with a large boyfriend in tow. I calmed him down and recounted the series of events from that night that had led him to my bar this night. To which he said to her, "You drank a shot while it was still on fire?" And then laughed ceaselessly. After she stormed out, he asked if he could buy me a shot. I replied, "Something on fire, maybe."

• KAGANO •

CHRISTIAN SUZUKI

S an Francisco's bar scene isn't only about the headliners who own the bars. It's quite the opposite actually. Our cocktail bars are filled with great talent, the ones actually making your cocktails, and they're often working at multiple bars at one time. That is how Christian Suzuki has gained incredible experiences from some of the greatest programs in the city, to the point that he can be a contender in major bar competitions and launched his very own bar pop-up. Kagano, by the way, is the name of that bar pop-up, along with something else that is very close to him and his family. "Kagano is the name of the cocktail bar my grandmother owned in Tokyo during the 50s and 60s," Suzuki explains. "During that time in Japan, not many women were seen in bars, let alone owning one. This cocktail was what led me to be National Finalist for Bacardi Legacy 2018."

GLASSWARE: Cocktail glass
GARNISH: Cut banana leaves and edible flower

- 1½ oz. Bacardi 8 Rum
- ½ oz. umesu
- ½ oz. blended scotch
- ¼ oz. banana liqueur
- 1 dash saline
- 1 slice of orange peel

1. Combine all of the ingredients, except the orange peel, in a mixing glass with ice, stir, and strain into the glass.

2. Express orange peel over the drink and discard. Garnish with banana leaves and an edible flower.

· RED TEMPLES ·

CHRISTIAN SUZUKI

For this cocktail, Christian Suzuki uses shochu as the base, then takes the drinker for a wild, yet elegant, ride full of fruit, bitter, nuttiness, floral notes, and smoke. It's got it all in beautiful harmony. That seems fitting with the inspiration coming from the magnificent Sensoji Temple in the Asakusa district of Tokyo, which is Suzuki's hometown.

GLASSWARE: Rocks glass

GARNISH: Smoked cinnamon stick

- 1 strawberry
- 1 oz. Iichiko Saiten Shochu
- ¾ oz. Campari
- ¾ oz. Amontillado Sherry
- ¼ oz. St. Germain Elderflower Liqueur
- 5 dashes peated scotch

1. Muddle the strawberry in a mixing glass.

2. Add the rest of the ingredients to the mixing glass with ice, stir, and double strain into the glass over ice (double straining this is important to prevent any strawberry pieces from going into the cocktail).

3. Torch one end of a cinnamon stick for garnish.

CHRISTIAN SUZUKI

Where *doesn't* Christian Suzuki work? If you've been to any of the top bars in San Francisco, I guarantee that you've encountered this star bartender. I first met him when Bon Voyage! opened in the Mission in 2018. He's also been the bar manager for Tradition (now Zombie Village) and assistant manager for 15 Romolo. As the COVID-19 pandemic struck, he was working shifts at Wildhawk, Elda, The Treasury, and Benjamin Cooper. I'm tired just thinking about that schedule. And he has his own pop-up, Kagano. I'm sure you'll be seeing a permanent bar from this ultra-talented bartender soon.

HOW DID YOU GET YOUR START IN BARTENDING AND DESIGNING DRINKS? ANY PARTICULAR MENTORS OR INFLUENCES THAT ARE STILL IMPACTFUL ON WHAT YOU DO TODAY?

I've always been in restaurant hospitality. I kind of grew up into it. My grandparents had a very well-known restaurant business in Tokyo. Their first restaurant, Aramasa opened right after World War II ended. Its focus was Northern Japanese cuisine. My grandfather got a lot of recognition for traveling back to Northern Japan to collect local ingredients and also using fresh produce and seafood. My grandparents together opened two more Aramasa locations, a teppanyaki steakhouse called Sukizuki, a ranch that sourced all of the company's produce and proteins, and of course, Kagano Bar—the cocktail bar my grandmother ran during the 50s and 60s. My grandparents would have me return to Japan up to three times a year from ages eleven to eighteen to study Japanese hospitality, food, and management, and then I moved there for over a year. During that time, I was trying to attend an art school in Tokyo but failed to get in. When I returned to the States, I wanted to get my foot into bar hospitality, so I applied for a job at 15 Romolo when I was twenty-one. There I went under the wings of Jared Anderson, Aaron Gregory Smith, and Ian Adams. They taught me to be the most excellent cocktail server, then manager, and then bartender. Ian Adams would always encourage me to study bakers and pastry chefs and how their knowledge in flavor pairings comes to fruition.

HOW WOULD YOU DESCRIBE YOUR DRINKS STYLE? OR IF STYLE ISN'T THE BEST ADJECTIVE, YOUR STRATEGY BEHIND BUILDING A COCKTAIL? THE SECRET TO THE CREATIVE SUCCESS?
My style would be Japanese-influenced, simple yet complex. I love being able to tell a story behind the cocktail.

BIGGER PICTURE NOW, YOU KNOW SAN FRANCISCO CRAFT COCKTAILS AS WELL AS ANYONE, WHAT IS IT THAT MAKES THIS CITY AND THE BAY AREA'S CONTEMPORARY COCKTAIL SCENE SO UNIQUE COMPARED TO OUR BIG CITY PEERS?
When I compare the craft cocktail scene in San Francisco to Chicago, Tokyo, New York, London, or Paris, I'd like to think that San Francisco's approach is a lot more conservative. There are so many incredible bars but a very small handful that have a crazy, experimental approach to cocktail development. Even when I go to smaller markets, like Portland, there are so many crazy and interesting things that are going on. I think that part of this is that at its core, San Francisco is about the purity of spirits. Hell, it was just ten years ago when every bartender in San Francisco was drinking straight Fernet Branca like it was filtered water!

AND AS A BARTENDER, YOU MUST BE SPOILED BY OUR YEAR-ROUND SEASONAL PRODUCE HERE?
So incredibly spoiled! We are so lucky to have programs that allow us access to them too! For example, CUESA (Center of Urban Education Sustainable Agriculture) puts on a few events a year where a bartender and a sponsored spirit brand are given access to all the common and unique produce that is being grown in Northern California so as to create a cocktail with them and serve them. I remember I was submitting a cocktail for a competition and was thinking about

strawberries. One of the brand folks let me know that strawberries may not be in season in the state where the competition was to take place. I was baffled!

WHEN YOU THINK OF SAN FRANCISCO COCKTAIL HISTORY, WHAT COMES TO MIND?
Many, many decades of many, many hangovers.

ANY STANDOUT LESSONS OR EXPERIENCES FROM THE MANY ACCLAIMED BARS YOU'VE WORKED AT, LIKE BENJAMIN COOPER, ELDA, AND 15 ROMOLO?
Not to be a square and be friendly. Those two mentalities behind the bar have helped me create so many incredible bonds with guests, co-workers, brand folks, and employers.

CORRIDOR

The Hi Neighbor Group's bustling spot right by City Hall, and the various concert halls and theaters, saw lots of changes in its early days—no cocktails, counter service only. Things have changed in the years since the opening days, as Corridor has found its stride as a power lunch spot by day, pre-show/post-work gathering spot for happy hour, then a wonderful cocktails-and-dinner spot as the sun sets . . .best enjoyed with Fernando Becerra's Sloe Sunset.

GLASSWARE: Tulip glass
GARNISH: Mint, paprika, and seasonal edible flower

- 1 oz. Hibiscus-Infused Rum
- ½ oz. sloe gin
- ½ oz. Pama Pomegranate Liqueur
- 1 oz. fresh grapefruit juice
- ½ oz. fresh lemon juice
- ½ oz. simple syrup

1. Combine all of the ingredients in a cocktail shaker, shake vigorously, and strain into the glass over crushed ice.

2. Garnish with mint, paprika, and a seasonal edible flower.

HIBISCUS-INFUSED RUM: Add 20 grams dehydrated hibiscus flowers to 1 liter silver rum and let stand at room temperature for 48 hours. Strain and store,

· W!TCH DOCTOR ·

THE LINDEN ROOM

Please don't bring seven of your friends to this Art Deco bar with eight seats. The Linden Room isn't San Francisco's smallest bar (supposedly The Black Horse London Pub has that title), but it is no doubt the city's most intimate high-end cocktail room. It's also attached to one of our great fine dining restaurants, Nightbird, where chef Kim Alter serves some of the most exciting, wonderfully composed tasting menus in the Bay Area. Diners there can enjoy The Linden Room's cocktails, while the bar's guests simply enjoy the drinks and can plan for dinner there later. The bar's drinks beautifully follow the ambitious, seasonal-minded blueprint of the food. To wit, this one was crafted by Chef Alter.

GLASSWARE: Rocks glass

- 1 sage leaf
- ¾ oz. Cognac (Comandon VS)
- ¾ oz. mezcal (El Mero Mero)
- ½ oz. Cocchi Torino
- ¼ oz. Cynar
- ¼ oz. maraschino liqueur
- 2 dashes grapefruit bitters
- Grapefruit peel, for expressing

1. Smoke the sage leaf in an upside-down rocks glass. Discard sage and add 1 large ice cube to the glass.

2. Combine all of the ingredients, except the grapefruit peel, in a mixing glass with ice, stir, and strain into the cocktail glass.

3. Express the grapefruit zest over the glass, then discard the peel.

· THE LAST STRAWBERRY ·

RICH TABLE

It isn't an easy task to create cocktails on par with the sensational, inventive seasonal cooking at Hayes Valley's Rich Table. The cooking is deeply complex, yet simultaneously fresh, satisfying, and comforting. Every time I visit the restaurant, I leave thinking, "Wow, if this isn't a perfect restaurant, then I don't know what is."

And it isn't just about the food in the serene space overlooking the frantic traffic of Gough Street. Larry Piaskowy's cocktails, like this elegant strawberry-centric creation, strike all the right notes in following the food's philosophy of letting a little creativity nudge peak seasonal ingredients to their full potential.

GLASS: Nick & Nora glass or coupe
GARNISH: Fresh strawberry wedge

- 1¼ oz. The Botanist Gin
- ¾ oz. Manzanilla sherry
- ¾ oz. Strawberry Syrup
- ¼ oz. fresh lemon juice
- 3 dashes orange bitters

1. Combine all of the ingredients in a cocktail shaker with ice, shake vigorously, and double strain into a Nick & Nora glass or coupe.

2. Garnish with the strawberry wedge.

STRAWBERRY SYRUP: Wash 1 pint strawberries and add them to a blender, greens included. Add 12 oz. rich simple syrup (2:1), and ¼ teaspoon salt to the the strawberries and puree. Fine strain and store in the refrigerator for 1 week, or freeze

LARRY PIASKOWY

RICH TABLE

Originally from the South Side of Chicago, Larry Piaskowy arrived in San Francisco right as the modern cocktail revolution was beginning at the turn of the 21st century. Before then, and since then, he's held pretty much every job that you could hold at a restaurant—server, dishwasher, chef, bar manager, bartender. He even designed the wine list for a restaurant that he and his wife had in Washington state. Piaskowy's San Francisco career has taken him all over town, from cooking at 15 Romolo to bartending at True Laurel, with stops at Alembic, with the Bon Vivants (at the now-closed Aatxe), and a whole lot more. Do you have a question about a San Francisco bar or restaurant? He has an answer. Now he's creating the cocktails for Rich Table, a Hayes Valley restaurant that is filled every night with diners enjoying the creative, fervently seasonal cooking expression of chefs Evan and Sarah Rich.

Larry and I chatted for an hour before a dinner service at Rich Table. Here are some of his takes on the cocktail world and the world at large.

ON DESIGNING COCKTAILS AT RICH TABLE . . .

The philosophy with how they run the restaurant fits with mine. They let me do whatever I want. I have complete autonomy—as long as my numbers are good. I come in and do what's best for the restaurant and try to make the best decision for the restaurant. I've been around long enough where I realize when it's my restaurant, it's my vision. I control it. When I work at Rich Table, it's Evan and Sarah's vision. So, I'm here to help their dreams come true.

They quite literally go to the market, find what's good, and cook it. So when something's out at the market, they change it. And it just made sense to me from the beginning to do the cocktails that way. I try to follow their lead. Whenever they bring anything from the market, I try to find a way to use that in cocktails. I've always been the kind of person who tried to use every part of the product, even before it was trendy. It's always been like we kill a pig, we eat the whole pig. I grew in Chicago near the back of the yards where they said they used everything except the oink.

AN EXAMPLE PIASKOWY-RICH TABLE COCKTAIL . . .

When citrus season started, they used a lot of pomelos and grape-fruits, so we did this grapefruit cocktail. I had them save me the trim from the fruits. I took that trim and made an oleo saccharum out of it. Now it's like, I have this oleo saccharum because instead of throwing the trim in the garbage I found a way to use it. It helps our food costs. It's good for everything. Then I wanted to do a gin cocktail and I just got introduced to this new gin called The Mast that's very grapefruit with cardamom and bay laurel. I knew this gin with this oleo saccha-rum was going to be brilliant! So I kind of built up the cocktail starting from the trim because I find my inspiration from ingredients, or some-times a spirit, or sometimes I drink something somewhere else or eat something and think "Oh, I want to work with that ingredient."

HOW DID YOU GO FROM A CHEF TO THE BAR SO EFFORT-LESSLY?

Part of my job as the chef was to make the shrubs and syrups and juices and all that stuff, so I had to work with the bartenders and take their wacky ideas for their cocktails and be able to put it into some-thing that I could actually produce in the kitchen at volume. Some-times they would come up with this syrup that made a cup and it's like, "Oh great, you took hours to make a cup of something. I need to figure out how to take the flavors you want for this cocktail and make two gallons of it in less time than that." So, I started learning how to work with bartenders as a chef and making a little bit more of a contri-bution to the bar than I had originally set out to because now I'm help-ing bartenders' ideas comes to fruition.

THE ALEMBIC'S FORMER BAR MANAGER ETHAN TERRY TRAINED YOU HOW TO OPERATE A BAR PROGRAM—AND YOU ALSO HELPED QUITE A BIT FROM THE CULINARY SIDE FOR COCKTAILS.

I would show up at his admin days on Mondays and see how he ordered, how he prepped his cocktails, and how he created the menu and worked through that. He would say like "I want to make a strawberry cocktail with black pepper." So I helped him not just put black pepper and strawberry in the cocktail but put a little Szechuan peppercorn and a little bit of chili flake, because black pepper fades over time. The chili flake helps keep that pop.

IF YOU HAVE 12 MEALS

How in the world do you choose where to drink in San Francisco? Well, that's a hard enough question with how many great bars we have. But—making a decision about what restaurants to visit when traveling here? That is even harder, given that we have hundreds, if not thousands of noteworthy places to eat. If I had to choose just a dozen meals to enjoy in San Francisco (and I sure hope that I'm never limited to that!), here is where I would go.

B. PATISSERIE
In a city filled with bakeries, start here for baguettes, kouign amanns, and about fifty other pastries and desserts.

CALIFORNIOS
Val M. Cantu's elaborate Mexican-influenced tasting menus are high-end dining at its most compelling.

DRAGON BEAUX
Stellar traditional and modern dim sum, closely followed by Hong Kong Lounge II and Yank Sing.

FLOUR + WATER
San Francisco's de-facto signature cuisine is "contemporary Italian" and this decade-old Mission spot is arguably the best example of that. Pastas here range from great to epic.

LAZY BEAR
Besides great cocktails, as you now know, the communal dining pop-up turned lavish prix fixe dinner spot is the most fun and arguably most exciting fine-dining splurge in the Bay Area.

NOPA
It's a classic debate—which came first, the restaurant Nopa or neighborhood NoPa (North of the Panhandle). Who cares, really, because Laurence Jossel's restaurant does everything so well, from late night burgers to weekend brunch, and a lot in between.

NOPALITO
Nopa's sibling always draws the crowds for pozole, margaritas, homemade tortillas, and lots of other highlights of regional Mexican cooking and agave spirit cocktails.

OCTAVIA
Out-of-towners think San Francisco is filled with little neighborhood restaurants that firmly toe the line of upscale and casual for food and

atmosphere, with fresh local produce always being the main driving force. The fact is that we don't have as many of those as you think. Luckily, Octavia in Lower Pacific Heights is one of them.

THE PROGRESS
A coin flip is needed for me to pick which of the two Stuart Brioza-Nicole Krasinski restaurants to include. The dim sum-style eating at ultra-popular State Bird Provisions? Or The Progress, a grand, wonderful restaurant in a former movie theater? The edge for me goes to The Progress because it's a little more refined and less hectic, and has very impressive cocktails.

RINTARO
Former Chez Panisse chef Sylvan Mishima Brackett's sheer focus on homemade ingredients and classical Japanese techniques for traditional and creative izakaya dishes is downright mind-boggling.

SWAN OYSTER DEPOT
As one of the few slices of old-time San Francisco remaining, the Sancimino family's seafood counter always has a line from before opening until closing. Every trip for Dungeness Crab Louie and fresh oysters will make your week much brighter.

ZUNI CAFÉ
The late chef/owner Judy Rodgers's roast chicken is quite possibly the city's most celebrated dish, but don't forget that this eclectic, always joyous and bustling Market Street restaurant is so good at so many things. The signature espresso granita dessert and lunchtime pizzas are gold standards in San Francisco, plus there's a knockout cocktail and wine program.

· SIMON SAYS ·

PLÄJ

Stockholm native Roberth Sundell quietly has made this hotel restaurant (it happens to be a great restaurant in a boutique hotel) in Hayes Valley one of the must-try dining destinations of the city. It also happens to be right by the opera, ballet, and symphony, so it's absolutely meant for a special pre-show bash. Toast to a night on the town, or the joys of herring and aquavit, with this fun raspberry-aquavit sour.

GLASSWARE: Coupe
GARNISH: Licorice Tincture

- 1¾ oz. California Aquavit
- ¼ oz. Maraschino liqueur
- 1 oz. egg white
- 1 oz. fresh lemon juice
- 1 oz. Raspberry Syrup

1. Combine all of the ingredients in a cocktail shaker and dry shake. Add ice and shake again.

2. Double strain into a coupe and garnish with 4 drops Licorice Tincture.

RASPBERRY SYRUP: Add equal parts fresh raspberries, sugar, and water to a saucepan over medium heat and simmer for 20 minutes. Fine strain and store.

LICORICE TINCTURE: In a container, combine 1 cup vodka with half a bag of Turkish Pepper Candy (a Swedish salted licorice candy), and a few drops of black food coloring. Let sit at room temperature for 48 hours, then strain and store.

· AIPUR EMERALD COCKTAIL ·

AUGUST 1 FIVE

Near City Hall and Hayes Valley, August 1 Five (August 15 is India's Independence Day from British rule) was an oasis of calm and dining joy slightly removed from two busy (and very different) areas. The restaurant just might have been the city's leading example of contemporary Indian cuisine, but it's the outstanding cocktails that really made August 1 Five one of the best restaurants in the city, period. Sadly, the restaurant closed during the COVID-19 pandemic.

GLASSWARE: Coupe

GARNISH: Orange flower

- 2 oz. tequila
- 1 oz. fresh lime juice
- ¾ oz. Khus-Cilantro-Thai Chili Syrup
- Coconut Foam, for topping

1. Combine all of the ingredients, except the foam, in a cocktail shaker with ice, shake vigorously, and double strain into a coupe.

2. Top with Coconut Foam and garnish with orange flower.

KHUS-CILANTRO-THAI CHILI SYRUP: Combine 1 liter khus syrup (available online or in specialty grocery stores), 1 bunch cilantro, and 5 Thai chilies in a blender and puree. Fine strain and store.

COCONUT FOAM: Add 10 oz. coconut milk, 5 oz. simple syrup, 10 oz. egg whites, 10 drops coconut extract, and ½ oz. saline to an ISI whip double charge with NO2. Shake well.

· BOOTLEGGER'S BARREL DRINK ·

TONGA ROOM & HURRICANE BAR

The irresistibly fun Tonga Room opened in 1945 in the stately Fairmont San Francisco Hotel on Nob Hill, is a global icon. You probably know about the rainstorms, the lagoon complete with a band performing on a thatched-roof barge, the incredibly detailed tiki décor. But here's what you also need to know: the drinks have evolved and are fantastic reflections of the present high-quality trends. Great ingredients, thoughtful and complex combinations, not too sweet—try this barrel and you'll understand.

GLASSWARE: Barrel mug

GARNISH: Lemon wheel and 2 bird's eye chilis

- ¾ oz. Bulleit Bourbon
- ¾ oz. Smith & Cross Rum
- ½ oz. Amaro Notion
- ½ oz. Ancho Reyes Liqueur
- ½ oz. passion fruit syrup
- ½ oz. fresh lemon juice

1. Combine all of the ingredients in a cocktail shaker with crushed ice, shake vigorously, and pour the contents into a barrel mug.

2. Garnish with lemon wheel and 2 bird's eye chilis.

HOTEL BARS

Who doesn't love a great airport bar or hotel bar? Unfortunately, SFO has just one good flight delay cocktail bar (at Tartine Manufactory in the International Terminal). Luckily, we have hundreds of hotels and a good number of them have excellent bars that are favorites of tourists and locals alike. In fact, some of our hippest and some of our most popular bars are actually in hotels. Just don't call them "hotel bars"; they're great bars in a hotel.

AMERICANO
The Hotel Vitale's bar is an excellent meeting place near the Ferry Building that manages to be relaxed-chic and dressed-up simultaneously, and one of the best bars for trying draft cocktails or frosé (all day!). Besides, how can a bar that shares a name with a famous cocktail not be great?

BAR AT HOTEL KABUKI
Excellent cocktails can be found at the main lobby bar of Japantown's stalwart boutique hotel, along with at the adjacent, highly acclaimed Thai restaurant, Nari, where Megan Daniel-Hoang creates exciting cocktails.

THE BIG FOUR
This is old-school San Francisco in its most luxurious state, complete with piano music and giant paintings of California's railroad barons, savored high atop Nob Hill in the Scarlet Huntington.

CHARMAINE'S
The San Francisco Proper Hotel's rooftop destination with drinks designed by the Bon Vivants is as close to A-list stylish/hip as it gets in this city.

DIRTY HABIT
Once you get past the weird "dirty" theme that seems more like corporate-speak than actual seduction, enjoy the contemporary, very in-

tricate drinks by Raul Ayala at what previously was one of San Francisco's most acclaimed fine dining restaurants (The Fifth Floor).

EVERDENE'S
Virgin Hotel SF's hip but not too-hip rooftop bar in SoMa has a relentlessly spectacular view of almost the entire Bay Area (and Bay Bridge traffic).

THE FISHER LOFT
There is so much history here at what was the Burritt Room and Tavern under different ownership, but the drinks, live music, and fun vibes are basically on the same level as before.

RITZ-CARLTON SAN FRANCISCO LOUNGE

It's a weird juxtaposition of stately Ritz-Carlton exterior then the chic design of its restaurant's bar and lobby lounge, but the excellent, usually complex drinks, really do put on the ritz.

THE PIED PIPER

The Palace Hotel has two landmarks: the grandiose Garden Court for overpriced but sumptuous brunch, and the intimate bar with the famous, eponymous Maxfield Parrish painting. Cocktails here can be decent but aren't always on the level of these other bars in hotels.

· SAILOR'S GUILLOTINE ·

TONGA ROOM & HURRICANE BAR

Chartreuse and absinthe in a tiki bar cocktail? Yes, it's a wonderfully orchestrated, albeit unexpected, cocktail. Enjoy, and I'm guessing you'll be singing with the band and me in the Tonga Room after the next "rainstorm."

GLASSWARE: Tiki mug

GARNISH: Mint and star anise

- ¼ oz. Raff Emperor Norton Absinthe
- 1 oz. La Favorite Agricole Rum
- ½ oz. Taylor's Falernum
- ½ oz. Green Chartreuse
- 1 oz. fresh pineapple juice
- ¾ oz. fresh lime juice

1. Combine all of the ingredients in a cocktail shaker with ice, shake vigorously, and pour into a tiki mug.

2. Top with crushed ice and garnish with mint and star anise.

· GREEN GOBLIN ·

THE SARATOGA

Bacchus Management is best known for their refined restaurants—Spruce in Laurel Heights and The Village Pub on the Peninsula. But for its Lower Nob Hill destination, the company decided to let uber-talented barman and partner Brandon Clements run the show with a cocktails-first approach (Spruce and The Village Pub have great cocktails but their wine programs are world-class). Clements has a particular affinity for Chartreuse, so take a wild guess what our cocktail selection features.

GLASSWARE: Coupe

GARNISH: Luxardo cherries

- 8 basil leaves
- 1 heaping teaspoon sugar
- 1¼ oz. Square One Botanical Vodka
- ½ oz. Green Chartreuse
- ¼ oz. Maurin Quina
- ¾ oz. fresh lime juice

1. In a cocktail shaker, gently muddle the basil leaves and the sugar.

2. Add the remaining ingredients to the shaker with ice, shake vigorously, and double strain into a chilled coupe.

3. Garnish with Luxardo cherries.

HORSEFEATHER

A pair of Future Bars alums set off on their own and designed this pretty much perfect relaxed bar, right in the heart of the exciting Divisadero corridor. Leave it to some of the city's most visionary cocktail minds to make celery, gin, and sauvignon blanc work together. It might even be healthy? Maybe or maybe not, but it certainly has staying power, having been on the menu since Horsefeather's opening in 2016.

GLASSWARE: Coupe

GARNISH: Thyme sprigs

- 1½ oz. dry gin
- ¾ oz. fresh celery juice
- ½ oz. Sauvignon Blanc Thyme Cordial
- ½ oz. fresh lime juice
- 1 oz. sparkling wine, Champagne preferred

1. Build the ingredients in a shaker tin (except the Champagne) and shake vigorously.

2. Fine strain into a coupe or a stemmed cocktail glass.

3. Top with Champagne and garnish with a few sprigs of thyme.

SAUVIGNON BLANC THYME CORDIAL: Add 1 (750 ml) bottle sauvignon blanc (choose a reasonably priced one that is dry with tropical and muscat notes) to a saucepan and bring to a light boil to begin cooking off the alcohol. Reduce heat and allow to simmer for 10 minutes. Add ½ bunch thyme and 1 small chunk horseradish, peeled and lightly crushed, and allow to infuse over low heat for 10 minutes. Add 1 quart sugar and stir to dissolve. Remove pan from heat and let stand until cooled. Remove thyme and horseradish, bottle, and refrigerate for up to 2 weeks (or add 1 oz. vodka to extend the shelf life to 3 weeks).

· ZOMBIE KILLER ·

LAST RITES

The Horsefeather team's dark tiki bar involves a crashed plane on a secluded tropical island—but no Wilson ball like in *Cast Away*. It takes guests less than two seconds to realize that Last Rites (from the same team as Horsefeather) is definitely not your average is-land-rum-tropical bar, nor are the drinks that skip any frilly, sweet-fruity direction. Here's a terrific version of the classic rum-heavy Zombie.

GLASSWARE: Tall collins or zombie glass
GARNISH: One pineapple frond, two cherries, and one pineapple triangle on a bamboo skewer topped with grated nutmeg

- 1¾ oz. overproof rum blend (consider a mix of Hamilton Navy Strength, Rumfire, Rum Bar Overproof, Wray and Nephew, and Smith and Cross)
- ¾ oz. Pink Zombie Mix
- ½ oz. fresh lime juice
- ½ oz. fresh pineapple juice
- ½ oz. coconut cream
- 1 dash absinthe

1. Build the ingredients in a mixing tin and add 5 oz. crushed ice.

2. Flash mix with a hand blender, then pour the mixture into a glass.

3. Garnish with pineapple frond, two cherries, and one pineapple tri-angle on a bamboo skewer topped with grated nutmeg.

PINK ZOMBIE MIX: In a container, combine equal parts of Cinnamon-Vanilla Syrup, velvet falernum, and grapefruit juice, mix well, and store.

CINNAMON-VANILLA SYRUP: Add 2 parts granulated sugar, ¾ part water, 2 Ceylon cinnamon sticks, and 1 vanilla bean to a saucepan over low heat. Bring to a simmer and stir constantly, until reduced to a syrup. Strain and store.

· TOUSSAINT 91 ·

LAST RITES

ather-son duo Calvin and Chase Babcock created this rum and clairin (also called "rum clairin") brand in 2017 to bring together their shared passions for Caribbean rum and the many charitable efforts their family has done with Haiti for four decades (Calvin practices medicine in Miami and co-founded the Living Hope Haiti movement). Chase resides here in the Bay Area, hence why their agricole-style rum clairin brand, Saint Benevolence, has already become an important back bar staple for many of our top bars. Rum clairin is Haiti's ancestral sugarcane spirit, and this particular one is exclusively made in the "Methode Saint Michel" (when some freshly-pressed sugarcane juice is turned into a syrup and fermented), which is the tradition of the Haitian village of Saint Michel where Saint Benevolence sources the hand-harvested sugarcane.

In addition, proceeds from the rum clairin (and Saint Benevolence's Caribbean 5-Year Rum Blend) go to Haitian charities—let's cheers to that.

This cocktail comes from Susan Eggett when she was working at Last Rites (now she's at Sobremesa). As history scholars might detect, it's named for Toussaint l'Ouverture, the leader of Haiti's 1791 Revolution, and is a unique take on a classic French 75.

GLASSWARE: Coupe

GARNISH: Dried lemon peel

- 1 oz. Saint Benevolence Rum Clairin
- ¾ oz. fresh lemon juice
- ¾ oz. rich simple syrup (2:1)
- 2 dashes Peychaud's Bitters
- 1 oz. Champagne, to top

1. Combine all of the ingredients, except the Champagne, in a cocktail shaker with ice, shake vigorously, and strain into a coupe.

2. Top with Champagne and garnish with dried lemon peel.

· PROPER CUP ·

CHARMAINE'S

When enjoying the view from the San Francisco Proper Hotel's glamorous rooftop hotspot, why not enjoy a clever riff on a Pimm's Cup?

GLASSWARE: Milkshake glass
GARNISH: Cucumber ribbon, lemon wheel, lime wheel,
apple slices, and mint sprig

- 2 oz. Pimm's
- ¾ oz. Hendricks Gin
- 1 dash Angostura Bitters
- 2 dashes Peychaud's Bitters
- ½ oz. fresh lemon juice
- ½ oz. fresh lime juice
- 1 oz. Apple Syrup
- Ginger beer, to top

1. Place two cucumber ribbons in a milkshake glass and set aside.

2. Pour all of the ingredients, except the ginger beer, into a cocktail shaker with ice, shake vigorously 20 times, strain into glass.

3. Fill the glass with ginger beer and garnish with lemon wheel, lime wheel, 2 apple slices, and 1 mint sprig.

APPLE SYRUP: Slice an apple and place it in a medium saucepan with 1 cup water, 1 cup sugar, and ½ teaspoon vanilla extract. Bring to a boil over medium heat, then turn down to medium-low and simmer for 5 minutes. Allow the syrup to cool and strain into a glass jar. Use at room temperature or refrigerate.

· THE SAN FRANCISCO TREAT ·

FISHER LOFT, PALIHOTEL SAN FRANCISCO

Film noir fans, here's looking at you kids. Burritt Alley, near Union Square, is where a plaque commemorates the scene from the *The Maltese Falcon*, when "Miles Archer, Partner of Sam Spade, Was Done In By Brigid O'Shaughnessy." It's that Burritt reference that inspired the modern-vintage second-floor hotel bar, Burritt Room + Tavern, which was one of the leading bars of the city's 2000s craft cocktail movement, thanks to Kevin Diedrich and later the Charlie Palmer Group. The jazz-filled, modern saloon vibe continues to this day on a high note as ownership changes turned the Burritt Room into Fisher Loft. Banana and Fernet Branca? It isn't a natural pairing but works wonders in this Fisher Loft creation.

GLASSWARE: Nick & Nora glass
GARNISH: Lime wheel and cocktail cherry

- 1½ oz. white rum
- ¾ oz. Crème de Banane
- ¼ oz. Fernet Branca
- ½ oz. fresh lime juice
- 1 bar spoon simple syrup
- 3 dashes chocolate bitters

1. Combine all of the ingredients in a cocktail shaker with ice, shake vigorously, and strain into a Nick & Nora glass.

2. Garnish with a lime wheel and cocktail cherry.

ABSINTHE BRASSERIE & BAR

The Absinthe Group's classic French flagship in the heart of bustling, chic Hayes Valley can safely be considered *the* place (or at least one of a tiny number in the late 1990s) where the modern cocktail movement started in San Francisco. Absinthe's bar program is all about classic cocktails, both beloved and forgotten, plus lots of Champagne—it's one of the most important pre- or post-opera and symphony spots after all, so festive bubbles are needed! Here's a smooth, lovely stirred bourbon drink that is the perfect nightcap after a show.

GLASSWARE: Double rocks glass

GARNISH: Grapefruit twist

- 2 oz. bourbon
- 1 oz. Punt e Mes
- ¼ oz. Burly Cascara Cola Syrup
- ¼ oz. Absinthe Verte
- 2 dashes Angostura Bitters
- 2 dashes orange bitters

1. Combine all of the ingredients in a mixing glass with ice, stir, and strain into glass over a single large ice cube.

2. Garnish with a grapefruit twist.

SMUGGLER'S COVE

Your home bar might not have the waterfalls and spectacular rum collection of Martin Cate's world renowned-rum paradise on Gough Street in Hayes Valley. Luckily, with a few syrups, a black blended rum, and a big ol' tiki mug, you can certainly produce this delightful Cate creation. In his words: "This drink is called The Expedition, and it's a celebration of the ingredients that Donn Beach, the godfather of tiki, was exposed to and celebrated—coffee and bourbon from New Orleans, fresh citrus from California, and rum and spices from the Caribbean."

GLASSWARE: 16 oz. tiki mug
GARNISH: Edible orchid

- 2 oz. black blended rum (such as Coruba, Gosling's, or Hamilton 86)
- 1 oz. bourbon
- ¼ oz. Bittermens New Orleans Coffee Liqueur
- 1 oz. fresh lime juice
- ½ oz. SC Cinnamon Syrup
- ½ oz. SC Honey Syrup
- ¼ oz. SC Vanilla Syrup
- 2 oz. seltzer

1. Add all the ingredients to a drink mixer tin with 12 oz. crushed ice and 4 to 6 small "agitator" cubes. Flash blend the mixture.

2. Open pour with gated finish into a mug or glass.

3. Garnish with edible orchid.

SC CINNAMON SYRUP: Add 2 cups water and 3 (6-inch) cinnamon sticks, halved, to a saucepan over high heat and bring to boil. When the water boils, add 4 cups granulated sugar and whisk until dissolved, about 1 minute (the liquid should become clear such that you can see the bottom of the pot). Immediately remove from the heat. Cover and let sit at room temperature for 12 hours. Strain through cheesecloth into a bowl and then use a funnel to pour into a lidded bottle or other sealable container. The syrup will keep, refrigerated, for several weeks.

SC HONEY SYRUP: Add 1½ cups honey to a saucepan over medium heat and warm until runny and not viscous—nearly to a boil but not quite. Add 1½ cups water to the hot honey and whisk together. Immediately remove from the heat. Let cool and store in a lidded bottle or other sealable container in the refrigerator. The syrup will keep, refrigerated, for several weeks.

SC VANILLA SYRUP: Add 2 cups water to a saucepan over high heat and bring to a boil. When the water boils, add 4 cups granulated sugar and whisk until dissolved, about 1 minute (the water should become clear such that you can see the bottom of the pot). Immediately remove from the heat. Halve 2 (8-inch) vanilla bean pods lengthwise and scrape the seeds into the syrup. Cut the scraped pods into thirds and add to the syrup. Stir well. Cover and let sit at room temperature for 12 hours. Strain through cheesecloth into a bowl. Pour through a funnel into a lidded bottle or other sealable container. The syrup will keep, refrigerated, for several weeks.

MARTIN CATE

It's hard to imagine a San Francisco without Smuggler's Cove, but the Hayes Valley rum and tiki bar only opened in 2009. Fun trivia: the location's predecessor was Jade Bar, where Rich Table's Larry Piaskowy once was the executive chef, along with at its neighboring sibling restaurant, Indigo. In the decade-plus since Martin Cate unveiled Smuggler's Cove, it has in many ways become the most prominent rum-centric cocktail bar in the country and possibly in the whole world. It fits the perfect balance of island paradise/tiki atmosphere without the kitsch, mixed with a fanatical reverence for rum's many dimensions and deep history. Smuggler's Cove, simply put, is Cate's great thesis about rum. Then in 2015, Cate's scholarly slant toward rum set the stage for a deep-dive focus on gin at Whitechapel near City Hall, which he opened with partners Alex Smith and John Park. Beyond the bars, Cate is an accomplished author, speaker, and ambassador for the world of rum—in many ways, one of the first true celebrity bartenders of the 21st century.

· ASYLUM HARBOR ·

WHITECHAPEL

For Martin Cate's second bar in San Francisco, which he opened with bartender Alex Smith and restaurateur John Park, gin is the spirits theme amidst the backdrop of a grand, almost ominously neglected Victorian era London Underground station—decidedly more aesthetically pleasing than our actual underground stations in San Francisco. Mind the gap when entering and enjoy one of San Francisco's (and one of the country's) most impressive collections of gins and gin cocktails. The cocktails vary dramatically in style, so one round will barely make a dent in the breadth of what Whitechapel offers. Many guests opt for the Asylum Harbor, one of the bar's most-ordered cocktails, which veers away from London for inspiration and heads toward the tropics.

GLASSWARE: Collins glass

GARNISH: Mint sprig and grapefruit twist

- 1¼ oz. Damrak Gin
- ½ oz. Benedictine
- ¼ oz. almond liqueur
- 1 bar spoon allspice dram
- ½ oz. ginger syrup

- ½ oz. passion fruit purée
- ½ oz. fresh lime juice
- ¾ oz. grapefruit juice
- Peychaud's Bitters, to top
- Freshly grated nutmeg, to top

1. Combine all of the ingredients, except the bitters and nutmeg, in a cocktail shaker with ice, shake vigorously, and strain into Collins glass.

2. Top with bitters and nutmeg and garnish with a mint sprig and grapefruit twist.

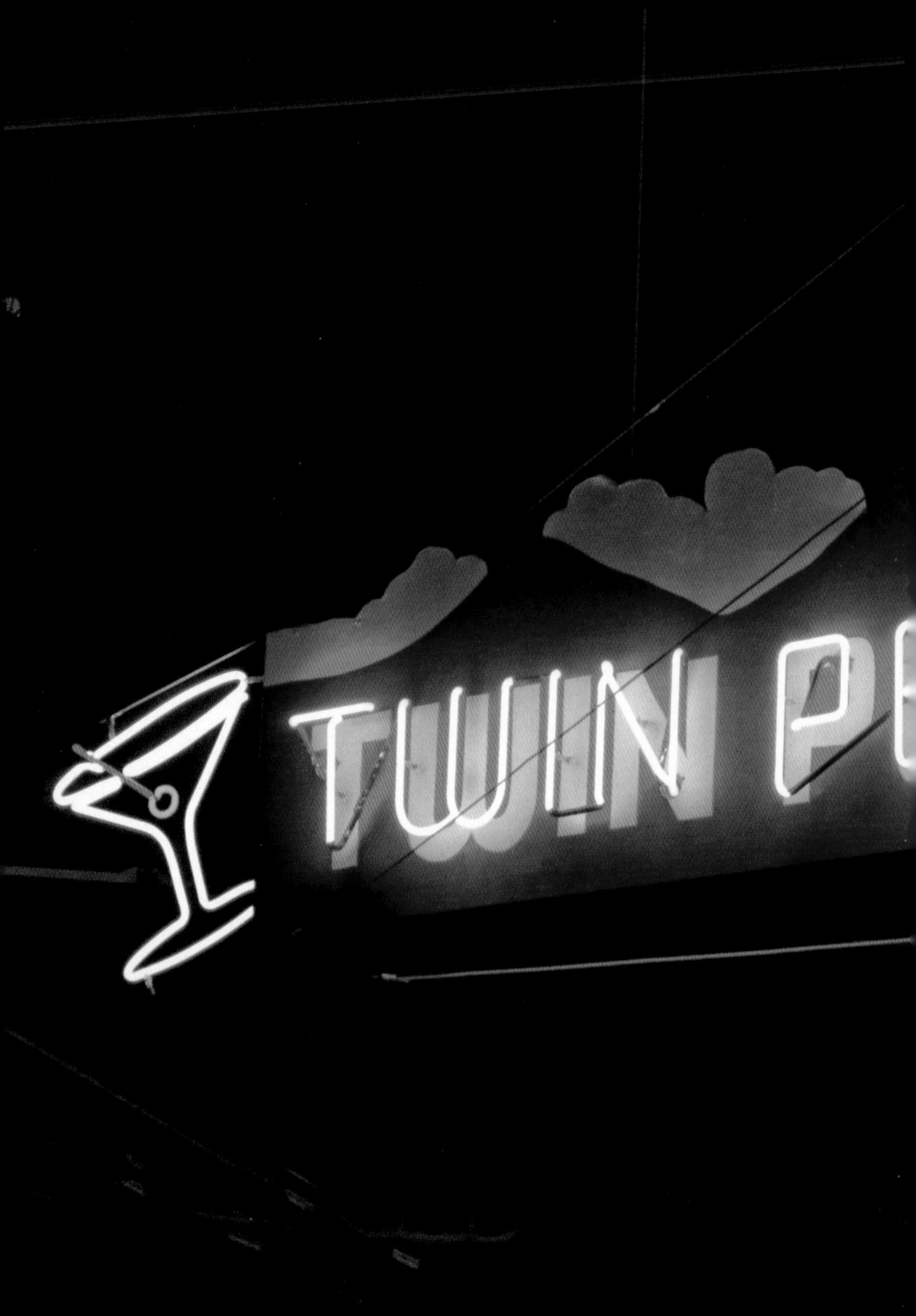
TWIN P

HISTORIC SAN FRANCISCO LGBTQ BARS

San Francisco's extensive LGBTQ history is a pivotal part of the city's bar history. Sadly, some of the longtime favorite gay and lesbian bars have closed, but there are still a number of beloved gathering spots that are constantly filled with both first-time visitors and regulars. A number of the great Castro nightlife spots, like Beaux and The Cafe, are really more nightclubs than bars, so we've focused here on the destinations that are truly bars. Some are on the older side, some are piano bars with giant-sized flavored martinis (Martuni's), and when it comes to historic bars and fun patios, there's no better duo than El Rio and Wild Side West.

Aunt Charlie's

Cinch

El Rio

Lone Star

Martuni's

SF Eagle

Twin Peaks

Wild Side West

THE AVENUES, NOPA, PACIFIC HEIGHTS,

COW HOLLOW, MARINA & PRESIDIO

TAMARINDO

MARTINI (SMOKED)

IN THE DAY WE GO ON FOREVER

INTERNATIONAL ORANGE

CLOVER CLUB

SALT & PEPPER

AZIZA

VIOLET SKIES

HABITUAL LINE STEPPER

CROSSOVER OLD FASHIONED

CLOSE BUT NO CIGAR

BARREL-AGED WHITE NEGRONI

MUCHO ALOHA

FORTUNATO'S REVIVER

M any San Franciscans arrived in the city because they were told to "Head West!" Well, you can't go much further west than these neighborhoods. The Presidio (a former military area) and Golden Gate Park take up much of this part of the city, functioning as necessary green spaces for busy city residents. NoPa's Divisadero Street resides at the east edge of the park and is home to many must-try restaurants and bars (and Alamo Square Park's famous view of the Painted Ladies Victorian homes). Divisadero and the parallel Fillmore Street both head steeply uphill to Pacific Heights, a neighborhood of extravagant homes, and views. Heading west, Cow Hollow's Union Street and the Marina's Chestnut Street are two more ultra-popular, upscale shopping, eating, and drinking areas. And then as far west as you can go are the "Avenues," named because of the easy-to-navigate numerical avenues. They are very quiet from the frequent chilly fog (nicknamed Karl the Fog by locals) and from being predominantly residential. The Avenues are generally divided into four neighborhoods: Outer Richmond, Inner Richmond, Outer Sunset, and Inner Sunset.

· TAMARINDO ·

CHE FICO

This multi-part creation from one of San Francisco's bartending all-stars is indeed complex, yet also not as stiff a challenge to produce as it initially seems—much like how Che Fico the restaurant is so daunting to get into (it's still near impossible to get a reservation after two years), but is just so darn relaxed and fun once you're inside. Christopher Longoria made Polk Street's 1760 a citywide cocktail favorite and now he's taken over another busy street, Divisadero, by the storm of his cocktails' force. Longoria's Tamarindo is a perfect pairing for the quirky, delightful pineapple pizza (I absolutely love it) and outstanding pasta from Che Fico chef David Nayfeld.

GLASSWARE: Large tumbler

- • 2 oz. Tamarindo Batch
- • 1 teaspoon Tamarindo Paste
- • ½ oz. fresh lemon juice

1. Combine all of the ingredients in a cocktail shaker with ice, shake for 8 seconds, and strain through a sieve into a large tumbler.

2. Add pebble ice and a straw.

3. Optional ¾ oz. House of Angostura Amaro sidecar can be poured on the cocktail.

TAMARINDO BATCH: Combine 5 oz. bourbon, 2½ oz. Jelinek Fernet, 2½ oz. Pimm's # 1, 2½ oz. Ginger Syrup, 1¼ oz. Giffard Orgeat, and 1 teaspoon Sibona Camomilla in a mixing glass and stir for 30 seconds.

TAMARINDO PASTE: In a large ziplock bag, combine 1 oz. orange peel (expressed), 3 oz. Zacapa 23 Rum, 6 oz. brown sugar cubes, 9 oz. hot water, and 14 oz. tamarind paste. Seal the bag. Carefully massage the bagged ingredients until they become a homogeneous texture. Let sit in a refrigerator for at least 24 hours.

GINGER SYRUP: Add 1 cup water, 1 cup granulated sugar, and ¾ cup peeled and thinly sliced ginger to a saucepan over medium heat and bring to a simmer, stirring until sugar is dissolved. Allow to simmer gently, uncovered, for 30 minutes. Remove from heat and strain through a sieve. Let cool to room temperature.

· MARTINI (SMOKED) ·

THE PROGRESS

Shaken or stirred? Many San Franciscans, myself included, prefer our martinis to be *smoked*, then stirred. It's the standout must-order at The Progress, an exciting yet relaxed higher-end restaurant (similar to State Bird Provisions next door). Stuart Brioza and Nicole Krasinski (he does the savory, she does the desserts) are two of the most gifted chefs in the city and both restaurants prove it. Which of the two Fillmore restaurants should you go to? Well, you have only one choice for this martini: The Progress.

GLASSWARE: Coupe
GARNISH: Smoked Castelvetrano olive

- 2½ oz. either gin or vodka
- ¾ oz. dry vermouth
- ¼ oz. Smoked Castelvetrano Olive Juice
- 8-10 drops Rosemary Oil

1. Combine all of the ingredients in a mixing glass with ice, stir, and strain into a coupe.

2. Garnish with a smoked Castelvetrano olive.

SMOKED CASTELVETRANO OLIVE JUICE: Smoke olives in their juice in a smoker box.

ROSEMARY OIL: Add grapeseed oil to a saucepan, heat it up until fish eyes appear, and remove from heat, steep fresh rosemary in it for 2 hours.

THE INTERVAL AT LONG NOW

One of San Francisco's most unique bars (of the many, many unique bars) is The Interval, located in the Long Now Foundation at Fort Mason, an old Army post that is now filled with arts and food companies. The bar includes a floor-to-ceiling library of books and mechanical prototypes to help civilization prosper deep into the future. On cue, the bar's menu tends to dabble in various time periods. This drink comes from the Postmodernism section of the menu and is based on Jeannette Winterson's Napoleonic Wars story, *The Passion*.

GLASSWARE: Wine glass

- • 2 oz. Giavi Prosecco
- • 1½ oz. LeMorton Pommeau
- • ½ oz. Amaro Montenegro
- • ¼ oz. fresh lemon juice
- • 1 oz. soda
- • ¼ oz. Small Hand Foods Passion Fruit Syrup

1. Add all of the ingredients to a wine glass with 5 ice cubes and stir.

BARS WITH A VIEW

Let's face it—San Francisco is a beautiful city! Why wouldn't we want to enjoy a cocktail with a view of the Bay Bridge or the Marin Headlands? Yes, these view bars can be touristy or cliché, but we actually have a fair number of places where the drinks are at least almost as special as the view, and these are some seriously special views that we're talking about here.

CHARMAINE'S AND EL TECHO AT LOLINDA
I'd vote in that order for the combination of view and high-quality cocktails. But, as the lines in rain or shine prove, all three of these rooftop bars have found the magic formula of stellar views with good-to-very good drinks.

THE HI-DIVE
Practically under the Bay Bridge, the patio of this Embarcadero classic is San Francisco's happiest happy hour. And I can't recommend enough to make this a Giants pregame spot.

MERSEA
Wait, Treasure Island? Yes, Treasure Island's low-key, high-quality, family-friendly restaurant boasts a breathtaking view of the city skyline, and actually does have a "you're on an island, relax" type of feeling that isn't possible on either side of the Bay Bridge.

THE RAMP
The Warriors' new Chase Center is mostly surrounded by apartments and medical buildings—and this awesome waterfront spot. With not much in the way of décor, The Ramp knows how to remind San Franciscans to chill, enjoy a Bloody Mary, and absorb the beauty of San Francisco Bay.

TOP OF THE MARK
At the top of the Intercontinental Mark Hopkins Hotel on the crest of Nob Hill, this old bar is Classic with a capital "C." I wish the drinks would step up slightly, but the view is outrageously beautiful.

VIEW LOUNGE
Herb Caen called the San Francisco Marriott Marquis the "jukebox" for its glass-enclosed design and the main song in that jukebox is The View Lounge on the top floor! Snacks and drinks are surprisingly enjoyable for a place that could totally coast on its magnificent view.

WATERBAR/EPIC STEAK
It's almost unfair how perfect the view is of the Bay Bridge from this high-end carnivore/seafood duo. Drinks are good, especially on the wine side, but you're coming for drinking in the view.

· INTERNATIONAL ORANGE ·

THE INTERVAL AT LONG NOW

The Golden Gate Bridge has long been a muse for local chefs and bartenders. With The Interval's proximity to the great bridge, it's only fitting that there is a cocktail nod to the orange (it is not actually golden) bridge. "This is my paean to the Golden Gate Bridge, at which our guests can gaze longingly, if not lovingly, from the Interval's back room," as beverage director and lead bartender Todd Carnam explains it.

GLASSWARE: Coupe

- 2 oz. 209 Sauvignon Blanc Barrel-Aged Gin
- 1 oz. Cocchi Torino
- ¼ oz. Gran Classico

- 2 dashes Angostura Bitters
- 1 dash orange bitters
- 5 drops salt solution (1:1)
- Lemon twist, for expressing

1. Combine all of the ingredients in a mixing glass with ice, stir to 32°F, and strain into a chilled coupe.

2. Express the lemon twist then discard.

· CLOVER CLUB ·

THE INTERVAL AT LONG NOW

As you have probably guessed by now, San Francisco is not as driven by old-school cocktails as cities like London and New York. That doesn't mean we don't like timeless classic cocktails or appreciate them. Appropriately for a bar focused on the future, this is a pre-Prohibition classic from The Interval named after the exclusive Philadelphia men's club—not named for Julie Reiner's excellent Brooklyn cocktail bar, though let's also give her credit for rekindling the world's excitement in this cocktail.

"In our version, we substitute Blanc vermouth for Dry, and Old Tom gin for classic London dry, resulting in a cocktail much more aligned, as I see it, along the axis it wants to travel," says Todd Carnam.

GLASSWARE: Coupe
GARNISH: Freshly grated nutmeg

- 1½ oz. Hayman's Old Tom Gin
- ½ oz. Dolin Blanc
- ¾ oz. fresh lemon juice

- ¾ oz. Small Hand Foods Raspberry Gum Syrup
- ½ oz. egg white

1. Combine all of the ingredients in a cocktail shaker with 1 ice cube and shake vigorously until dissolved. Add 3 more cubes and shake again for about 8 seconds.

2. Double strain into a chilled coupe and garnish with the nutmeg.

WILDSEED

We all know that cocktails are great for the spirit, but are they actually good for you? That's a topic for another book. However, I can diplomatically say that some cocktails certainly have more virtuous values than others, just like with any food or drink. This cocktail fits that profile, coming from one of San Francisco's most important restaurant openings of 2019. It's a sign of the times in our wellness-minded, global climate-conscious world, how the Cow Hollow restaurant Wildseed has a plant-based menu and makes it a point to serve only vegan wines (no egg fining). How do cocktails fit in this equation? Obviously, there won't be any egg white in that sour. You'll see a menu slanted toward fresh juices, fewer sweet elements, and ingredients that might even help cut down on aches, pains, and inflammation (and maybe even hangovers?). The work by Lauren Fitzgerald on this cocktail program with an overarching wellness emphasis is downright impressive.

GLASSWARE: Rocks glass

- Salt and pepper, for rim
- 1½ oz. Pueblo Viejo Blanco Tequila
- ½ oz. Quiquiriquí Espadin Mezcal
- ¼ oz. Ginger
- ⅛ oz. Turmeric
- ¾ oz. agave simple syrup (1:1)
- 3 drops ginseng tincture
- ¾ oz. fresh lemon juice
- ¼ oz. Habanero Vinegar (optional)

1. Rim one side of rocks glass with salt and pepper.

2. Combine all of the ingredients in a cocktail shaker with ice, shake vigorously, and strain into the rocks glass over ice.

GINGER: Combine a 1:3 ratio of ginger to water, then strain through fine mesh. Refrigerate.

TURMERIC: Combine a 1:3 ratio of turmeric to water, then strain through fine mesh. Refrigerate.

HABANERO VINEGAR: Add 6 habaneros (stems cut off but seeds left in), 2 cups white vinegar, and 1 teaspoon salt to a blender and blend on high. Fine strain through a chinoise. Refrigerate.

· AZIZA ·

FLAVOR BASKET

After a multi-year renovation, Mourad Lahlou's Outer Richmond Moroccan-Californian standout returned in 2019 and is as great as ever. Cocktails created at the restaurant's chic bar continue to be some of the city's most compelling (along with dishes from the kitchen like hand-rolled couscous and basteeya). The Flavor Basket is a great example of the bar's imaginative work, using a little-known Italian rose petal liqueur, aquavit, and gin, then finishing with a slight tiki/mai tai flair.

GLASSWARE: Coupe

GARNISH: Dehydrated lime wheel and seasonal flowers

- 3 oz. Batch
- ½ oz. orgeat
- ¾ oz. fresh lime juice
- 4 dashes Peychaud's Bitters
- Banana mist (can use banana liqueur and an atomizer)

1. Combine all of the ingredients, except the banana mist, in a cocktail shaker with ice, shake vigorously, and fine sieve into the coupe.

2. Spray the drink with banana mist and garnish with dehydrated lime wheel and seasonal flowers.

BATCH: In a large jar or bottle, combine 2 cups Uncle Val's Gin, ½ cup Italicus Bergamotto, and ½ cup Ahus Aquavit and mix well.

VIOLET'S

Bartenders across the Bay Area adore butterfly pea flower for its Instagram-friendly purple hue. So, if you're a restaurant named Violet's, it certainly makes sense to add some butterfly pea flower to a namesake cocktail. This Outer Richmond modern tavern's strong cocktail program is split between House Classics that have fun twists on old-school cocktails and Violet's Originals, which push the envelope with techniques and fresh ingredients (both pair beautifully with one of the city's best burgers and bowls of bar nuts). The Violet Skies comes from the former category, taking a classic Aviation for a flight with mezcal and coconut liqueur.

GLASSWARE: Coupe
GARNISH: Edible flower

- ¾ oz. Butterfly Pea Flower-Infused Del Amigo Mezcal
- ½ oz. Hood River Distillers Lewis & Clark Lookout Northwest Gin
- ½ oz. Ventura Spirits Strawberry Brandy
- ¼ oz. Kalani Coconut Liqueur
- ¼ oz. Rothman & Winter Crème de Violette
- ½ oz. fresh lemon juice
- 2 dashes Scrappy's Grapefruit Bitters

1. Combine all of the ingredients in a cocktail shaker, shake vigorously, then add ice. Shake until well-chilled.

2. Double strain into a chilled coupe and garnish with an edible flower.

VIOLET'S

Think autumnal martini here. Violet's certainly has quite the smart palate to figure out that combining pumpkin, tequila, oxidative notes of brandy, and sherry yields a fascinating toast-heavy flavor profile that evokes the sweater-wearing, leaves-on-the-ground sensation of a November day.

GLASSWARE: Nick & Nora glass

GARNISH: Cilantro leaf

- 1 oz. Pumpkin Oil-Washed Partida Reposado Tequila
- ¾ oz. Alma de Trabanco Quinquina
- ⅓ oz. Glasshouse Trade Winds Brandy
- ½ oz. Karabakh Apricot Brandy
- ½ oz. Grant Amontillado Sherry
- 2 dashes Bittercube Bolivar Bitters

1. Combine all of the ingredients in a mixing glass with ice, stir until well chilled, and strain into a Nick & Nora glass.

2. Garnish with a cilantro leaf.

PUMPKIN OIL-WASHED TEQUILA: In a large jar with a lid, combine 1 (750 ml) bottle Partida Reposado Tequila and 3 tablespoons La Tourangelle Toasted Pumpkin Seed Oil. Seal the jar and let stand in a dark, cool spot for 5 days. After the aging period, place the jar in the freezer and leave for 12 hours, or until the oil is well congealed. Strain the mixture through a coffee filter to remove all the oil from the tequila. If there are globules of oil left, refreeze and strain again until the tequila is free of oil. Bottle and use.

· CROSSOVER OLD FASHIONED ·

VIOLET'S

The most popular drink at Violet's is named for a nearby road through Golden Gate Park. It really is the perfect, smooth whiskey-forward pick-me-up after a chilly walk to see the windmills and bison.

GLASSWARE: Rocks glass

GARNISH: Lemon peel

- 1 oz. Rittenhouse Rye
- ½ oz. Wyoming Bourbon
- ½ oz. Comandon VS Cognac
- ¼ oz. Cardamaro
- ¼ oz. simple syrup
- 2 dashes Angostura Bitters
- 1 dash Scrappy's Black Lemon Bitters

1. Build in a rocks glass over a large ice cube, stir to incorporate all of the ingredients, then strain into a clean rocks glass.

2. Garnish with an expressed lemon peel.

THE COMMISSARY

Traci des Jardins's Spanish-Californian restaurant in the Presidio (the Presidio was a military outpost for three countries: US, Mexico, and Spain) tied together some late 1700s California history with the present. As a nod to the Presidio's early period under Spanish rule, there were plenty of sherries and sherry cocktails offered at The Commissary. Here's bar manager Anthony Stewart: "This is one of the first cocktails I put on the menu at The Commissary, and one of my favorites. I love this drink because it is a lighter version of an Old Fashioned, approachable and easy to drink. The Manzanilla Sherry is such a great ingredient and really ties in the Spanish direction of our menu as well as a nod to the Spanish heritage of the Presidio." Unfortunately, The Commissary closed permanently during the COVID-19 pandemic.

GLASSWARE: Rocks glass
GARNISH: Orange peel

- Laphroaig Scotch, to rinse
- 1 oz. Sagamore Rye
- 1 oz. Rittenhouse Rye
- ¾ oz. Bodegas Hidalgo Manzanilla Sherry
- ½ oz. honey
- 3 dashes Peychaud's Bitters

1. Spray a rocks glass with Laphroaig to rinse and add ice.

2. Combine the remainder of the ingredients in a mixing glass with ice, stir for 15 seconds, and fine strain into the rocks glass over ice.

3. Garnish with an orange peel.

· BARREL-AGED WHITE NEGRONI ·

PRESIDIO SOCIAL CLUB

The mid-20th century vibe and menu of the Presidio Social Club balanced the fine line of feeling like Eisenhower could be president, yet also having today's emphasis on all the relevant high-quality ingredients. Two of the modern cocktail world's hippest trends (bitter aperitivos and barrel-aging) converge in the Barrel-Aged White Negroni. You don't need a barrel for this drink, though, so don't let that get in the way. During the COVID-19 pandemic, PSC permanently transformed into the Presidio Social Club Exchange, yet still has those wonderful barrel-aged cocktails*.

GLASSWARE: Martini glass
GARNISH: Lemon twist

- 1 oz. Macaronesian White Gin
- 1 oz. Lillet Blanc
- 1 oz. Dolin Dry Vermouth

- 2 dashes Fee Brothers Grapefruit Bitters

1. Combine all of the ingredients in a mixing glass with ice, stir, and strain into a martini glass.

2. Garnish with a lemon twist.

This drink typically ages for about 6 to 8 weeks in a barrel (which holds 5 liters). Typically, an American Oak-Medium Toast barrel is used. You can buy a 1 liter barrel at Presidio Social Club. Or, use ¼ to ½ oz. soaked wood chips for every 1 liter of cocktail for the barrel aging if sans barrel.

· MUCHO ALOHA ·

ARGUELLO

With over 120 bottles of agave spirits (mezcal, sotol, tequila, and more!) on the menu of Traci des Jardins's Mexican restaurant in the Presidio Officers' Club, Andi Miller had no shortage of options when it came to agave toys to play with for cocktails. Del Maguey Vida Mezcal is the base of this unique clarified milk punch-pineapple cocktail. Unfortunately, Arguello closed permanently during the COVID-19 pandemic.

GLASSWARE: Rocks glass

- 2 oz. Del Maguey Vida Mezcal
- ½ oz. Plantation Pineapple Rum
- 1 oz. fresh lemon juice
- 1 oz. Pineapple Syrup
- ½ oz. simple syrup
- 3 dashes cinnamon or vanilla or chipotle bitters
- Whole raw milk

1. Combine all of the ingredients in a bowl, except the milk, and mix well.

2. Add the milk and allow it to curdle. Scale up to the desired amount of punch and add 20% of whole raw milk to total liquids, as well as water for desired dilution.

3. Refrigerate for 24, then strain through a fine cloth until a clear, shiny liquid is achieved. Serve.

PINEAPPLE SYRUP: Combine 1 part Pineapple Juice with 1 part Pineapple Water.

PINEAPPLE JUICE: Cut a fresh pineapple, reserving the skin and core. Chop the pineapple flesh. In a blender, liquify the pineapple and strain through a fine chinois.

PINEAPPLE WATER: Add the reserved pineapple skin and core, cinnamon sticks, whole chipotle, allspice, cloves, cacao nibs, and 6 quarts of water to a pot over low heat. Cook until the water is very fragrant. Strain and store in refrigerator.

THE ICE CREAM BAR

Who doesn't love a great soda fountain treat? Juliet Pries's excellent all things-ice cream destination in Cole Valley is beloved by all ages for myriad reasons, from malts and milkshakes to the 1930s soda fountain that was driven to San Francisco from its original home in Mackinaw City, Michigan. Plus, I can't forget the "remedies"—low-proof ice cream cocktail delights for the adults. Are they a dessert AND a cocktail? Or do they just count as one or the other, and it's okay to then also get a sundae or a beer? Whatever it is, my goodness is it delicious.

GLASSWARE: 12 oz. soda fountain tulip glass

GARNISH: Toasted black walnuts

- 1½ oz. Bodegas Yuste Aurora Amontillado Sherry
- ½ oz. Cocchi Vermouth di Torino
- ½ oz. rich turbinado simple syrup
- 3½ oz. vanilla ice cream
- 3½ oz. caramelized honey ice cream
- 3 tablespoons lightly toasted black walnuts, chopped

1. Combine all of the ingredients in a blender or milkshake maker and blend until smooth.

2. Pour into a chilled 12 oz. glass and garnish with toasted black walnut pieces.

NORTH BAY

GUERA

NIGHT VISION

VIOLETTA

TROPICAL DAIQUIRI 1898

CHOKE HOLD

SCORCHED ROSE

S.B.C

CUCUMBER MINT GIMLET

TIME'S ARROW II

ODE TO KIPLING

MAI TAI

NAVY GROG

86 DIGNITY

BALI SPICE OLD-FASHIONED

CUCUMBER COLLINS

For our definition of the North Bay, there are three counties to know: Napa, Marin, and Sonoma. Napa County is home to a certain wine-growing valley. Sonoma County is its neighbor to the west and extends all the way to a rugged, isolated Pacific Ocean coastline. You'll find vineyards, orchards, and farms all over Sonoma County. For my money, it's the greatest food and drink county in this country. Marin County is Sonoma County's southern neighbor, running all the way to the northern part of the Golden Gate Bridge. It's a vast county of eclectic towns, posh suburbs, and beautiful natural areas.

· GUERA ·

In the heart of apple and wine country, the Barlow in Sebastopol is a food and drink paradise of various restaurants, artisans, breweries, and more. Fern Bar is the resident cocktail bar, and it's a stunner both visually in the plant-filled space and with what you'll be served. This is their excellent take on a Paloma.

GLASSWARE: Collins glass
GARNISH: Grapefruit, lime wheel, and dehydrated grapefruit chip

- 1½ oz. Blanco Tequila
- 1 oz grapefruit juice
- ¾ oz. fresh lime juice
- ¼ oz. Aperol
- ¼ oz. St. Germain Elderflower Liqueur
- ¼ oz. Thai Pepper Shrub
- Fever Tree Bitter Lemon Soda, to top

1. Combine all of the ingredients, except the soda, in a Collins glass with ice, and stir.

2. Top with soda, to taste, garnish grapefruit and lime wheel down the side of the glass, and top with dehydrated grapefruit chip.

THAI PEPPER SHRUB: Add 4 roughly chopped up Thai or bird's eye chili peppers, ¼ cup cane vinegar, and ¼ cup cane sugar to a saucepan over medium-high heat. Bring to a boil for 5 minutes, let cool, and strain out the peppers.

· NIGHT VISION ·

DUKE'S SPIRITED COCKTAILS

Healdsburg is quite possibly California's quintessential wine country town. There are stellar wineries and tasting rooms, then acres and acres of vineyards in every direction—plus a cute central plaza in the "downtown" complete with a gazebo. One of the storefronts on the plaza happens to be Duke's, a cocktail bar treasure that is beloved by discerning cocktail drinkers, tourists who are tired of Zinfandel, and many wine and tourism industry workers who are looking to relax with a cold beer or a unique carrot-and-gin cocktail creation.

GLASSWARE: Cocktail glass
GARNISH: Fresh carrot frond

- 1½ oz. Spirit Works Barrel Gin
- 1 oz. Fresh Carrot Juice Syrup
- ½ oz. fresh lemon juice
- ¼ oz. Bordiga Extra Dry Vermouth
- 2 dashes Oloroso sherry
- 2 dashes Caraway Tincture

1. Add all of the ingredients to a cocktail shaker with ice, shake vigorously for 15 seconds, and double strain into a chilled cocktail glass.

2. Garnish with a fresh carrot frond.

FRESH CARROT JUICE SYRUP: Combine 2 parts fresh carrot juice to 1 part simple syrup.

CARAWAY TINCTURE: Steep 2 tablespoons caraway seeds in 4 oz. high-proof neutral grain alcohol for at least 24 hours, shaking periodically. Strain and store.

WINE PARADISE

Sorry cocktails, but there are some good local rivals when it comes to drink choices. The Bay Area has a very decent argument for being the wine capital of the world. Without traffic, San Francisco is one hour from the Napa Valley, Sonoma County, the Santa Cruz Mountains, and Livermore Valley. Plus, there are outstanding urban wineries in Oakland and Berkeley. And, hey, Lodi is just over an hour away, directly east of San Francisco.

Buena Vista opened in Sonoma in 1857 as the area's first main commercial winery, and the 1976 Judgement of Paris tasting helped Northern California wines soar to international attention after our wines defeated the supposedly unbeatable French wines in a prestigious blind tasting.

If you want to read up on Bay Area wine, I suggest Jon Bonné's *The New California Wine*. In the meantime, here's my cheat sheet for wineries in seven different regions. (Note that many require advanced reservations.)

Upper Napa Valley
Buehler
Chappellet
Corison
Failla
Larkmead
Seavey
Smith-Madrone
Spottswoode
Young Inglewood

Lower Napa Valley
Far Niente

Frog's Leap
Robert Sinskey
Saintsbury
Shafer
Trefethen
Tres Sabores
Y. Rousseau

Russian River Valley/Dry Creek Valley/Sebastopol
Cobb
Freeman
Littorai

MacRostie
Maurtison
Porter Creek
Preston
Reeve
Small Vines
Unti

Sonoma area
Hamel
Hanzell
Kivelstadt
Scribe
Talisman

Livermore Valley
3 Steves
Cuda Ridge
McGrail

Nottingham Cellars
Occasio
Page Mill

Santa Cruz Mountains
Alfaro
Byington
Cooper-Garrod
Thomas Fogarty
Ridge Montebello Estate
Wrights Station

Oakland/Berkeley
Blue Ox
Broc
Donkey & Goat
Maitre de Chai
Windchaser
Vinca Minor

· VIOLETTA·

COPITA

Any visit to Larry Mindel and Joanne Weir's Sausalito restaurant isn't complete without the legendary margarita to start and to learn about a new mezcal at some point in the meal. However, Copita has a whole wide world of exciting agave spirit cocktails to explore, like this nicely balanced—and bright purple—blanco tequila-based cocktail from Assistant General Manager Felix Barker.

GLASSWARE: Old Fashioned glass
GARNISH: Hibiscus flower and black lava salt rim

- 1 ½ oz. Maestro Dobel Blanco Tequila-Infused with Butterfly Pea Flower
- ½ oz. Crème de Violette Liqueur
- ½ oz. Giffard Pamplemousse Liqueur
- ½ oz. fresh lemon juice
- 1 oz. grapefruit juice

1. Rim an Old Fashioned glass with black lava salt.

2. Combine all of the ingredients in a cocktail shaker with ice, shake vigorously, and strain into the glass over a large ice cube.

3. Garnish with a hibiscus flower.

BUTTERFLY PEA FLOWER-INFUSED TEQUILA: Add ¼ cup butterfly pea flower to a 750 ml bottle of tequila and let stand for 1 day before using.

· TROPICAL DAIQUIRI 1898 ·

CALIFORNIA GOLD

Isaac Shumway's debut solo bar in San Rafael is cocktail gold for residents of Marin County, and within weeks garnered attention from the entire Bay Area (and even national award nominations). That's some big praise for what, at its core, is the long-needed community gathering spot for Marin's county seat. You'll want to order everything on the menu. So, I'll help out at least with the first order by letting Shumway describe his signature cocktail—I'll never call a three-ingredient cocktail "basic" ever again:

"I have had a daiquiri on every menu that I have ever put out because it is the foundation of my cocktail love and philosophy. With such simplicity in ingredients, I have to focus on the quality of the ingredients and techniques. For instance, something as classic and mainstream as a daiquiri, I had to really think about what makes a daiquiri special or stand apart. There are only three ingredients and beyond the recipe what else can be done? So I thought about each ingredient and how that affects the drink. Picking out the rum was the first thought. I feel strongly that the rum should be white so that the drink is clean, crisp, and lively. I went with the El Dorado because it has body, complexity, and vanilla notes. Through trial and error, I tried every sugar I could think of. Using raw sugars versus syrups, white or natural cane versus turbinado, Martinique Cane Syrup versus gum syrup. Then I started to blend sugar to get different flavors and textures. Then I thought about the lime, its oils and pith. The little bits of ice and lime that came though if you don't double strain. All of these have a huge effect on the end result of using only three ingredients."

GLASSWARE: Cocktail glass
GARNISH: Lime spiral

- 2 oz. El Dorado 3-Year Rum
- ½ oz. Sazerac Syrup

- 1 oz. hand-pressed lime juice with a half lime shell (no juice in the shell).

1. Add the rum and syrup to a cocktail shaker.

2. Hand squeeze a lime half to make 1 oz. of juice and add it to the cocktail shaker. Make sure you express all of the juice from the lime half and add the juice-less shell to the cocktail shaker.

3. Add ice and shake until the shaker is ice cold.

4. Single strain through a Hawthorne strainer, shaking out as much ice and lime that will fit through the Hawthorne into a chilled cocktail glass.

5. Garnish with a lime spiral.

SAZERAC SYRUP: First, make two different syrups. Evaporated Cane Simple Syrup is a 3:2 ratio of evaporated natural cane syrup and how water; stir to combine. Martinique Petite Canne Syrup is 1:1 ratio of Martinique petite canne sugar and water. Put the sugar in a saucepan with the water over heat, stirring and being careful not to let it come to a simmer. You only want to just warm this enough that the sugar is mostly dissolved. It will continue to dissolve over time after you take off the heat. You chemically change the taste of sugar if you heat this too much. You could also just use very hot water, stir, and wait until sugar fully dissolves. Mix the two syrups into a single syrup and store.

· CHOKE HOLD ·

CALIFORNIA GOLD

Reinterpreted classic cocktails are everywhere these days. At California Gold, Isaac Shumway has created a riff on the Brooklyn that has become even better known in the Bay Area than its classic inspiration. It's *that* good. Here's how he describes it:

"My Brooklyn variation using tequila! There are not enough stirred tequila cocktails out there in my opinion. It's such an exotic, beautiful spirit, made from Weber Blue Agave, which takes up to 5 to 8 years just to grow before distilling, resting, and aging. To give some perspective, the corn to make bourbon takes 8 to 10 weeks to grow. This relative of the thistle pairs beautifully with Cynar, which is a bittersweet amaro made from artichokes. Then add a little maraschino, which comes from Moraska cherries that are crushed up with the pits and stems, a little honey, Carpano Antica Formula Sweet Vermouth, and an orange peel."

GLASSWARE: Cocktail glass
GARNISH: Orange peel

- 1½ oz. Tapatio Reposado Tequila
- ¾ oz. Carpano Sweet Vermouth
- ½ oz. Cynar
- ½ teaspoon maraschino liqueur

1. Combine all of the ingredients in a mixing glass with ice, making sure that the ice is always above the line of the liquid. Stir until the contents are cold and strain into a chilled cocktail glass.

2. Express the oils of an orange peel over the drink. Drop the peel in and serve.

ISAAC SHUMWAY

CALIFORNIA GOLD

Like Larry Piaskowy (see page 205), Isaac Shumway is one of the few chefs-turned-cocktail masters who has risen through the ranks behind the bar to run their own program at a prestigious bar or to own their own bar. Shumway cooked at Bay Area fine dining stalwarts—The French Laundry, Masa's (now closed), Gary Danko—before shifting gears to the bar side. His bar career started with the best of the best—The Alembic, Bourbon & Branch, Heaven's Dog—before he was tasked with creating a revamped house cappuccino and full bar program for the new owners of the historic Tosca Cafe (see page 49). Then Shumway's career veered in another direction when he was tasked with opening the bar for Northern California's first Alamo Drafthouse, the Texas-based chain of movie theaters that actually pays lots of attention to high-quality food and drink. His journey then led him to neighborhood favorite Bloodhound in SoMa. Finally, the stage was set for his solo debut, California Gold, which opened in San Rafael in 2019. It is without question Marin County's definitive high-level cocktail bar.

HOW DO YOU GO FROM CHEF DE PARTIE AT THE FRENCH LAUNDRY TO BEING ONE OF THE MOST INFLUENTIAL BAR-TENDERS IN SAN FRANCISCO'S CRAFT COCKTAIL MOVEMENT?
I thought I was gonna go the distance with cooking. I left the Laundry to move in with my wife, girlfriend at the time. She wanted to be in San Francisco, so we moved. I was cooking in the city, but one day I went into Alembic when it first opened and my mind was blown. I had never seen a cocktail bar like this. In fact, at that time I was very disappointed in the cocktail scene and would only drink cocktails at home.

It was a hobby of mine as long as I can remember to read old cocktail and bar books. Anyways, Alembic was making an Old Fashioned and Sazerac and Whiskey Sours the way I read about in old books. I had never seen a Kold Draft before and I was in love!

I wanted to be a part of it desperately. I drank there a lot and asked a lot of questions. I hounded Daniel Hyatt for a job there every week until he finally gave me a job. I remember one day, after my, like, seventh resume drop-off attempt, he said that if someone didn't leave soon he would kill them for me. He gave me a shot and said he didn't have a job for me, but to come in to do a stage and check things out. So I did and at the end of it he offered me a couple of shifts. Maybe the most exciting thing that had ever happened to me. That and when I got the job at the French Laundry. The rest is history.

WHO WERE SOME MAJOR INFLUENCES ON YOUR GROWTH IN THE COCKTAIL WORLD?

If Daniel Hyatt and Erik Adkins had a son, I think that would be me.

Daniel was kind of a genius savant. He knew a little about everything. He was truly gifted and brilliant. He taught me about his philosophy of creating cocktails. Respecting ingredients and making sure there was a point to putting them together. He also taught me to tie it all together with other mediums. The literature and playfulness of the menu he wrote along with the music he played. He would teach us how to play music and transition into other music that would make sense. The art of a playlist.

We would have weekly bar meetings, learning about the ingredients, from fortified wine to sour beers, to agricole rhum and Marc brandy. Alembic captured the history of classic cocktails but also pushed the edge with contemporary ones. Daniel wasn't afraid to break the rules and I soaked this all up and California Gold very much embodies all of this.

Erik Adkins taught me a broader sense of gracious hospitality. I learned cocktail techniques and proper balance. He taught me how important it is to hand press citrus to get all the oils and to only use fresh juice. He introduced me to Charles H. Baker and a world of hot climate cocktails and I fell in love. He taught me a lot about bar manager philosophies. We talked about pricing and pour cost. The cocktails that Erik Adkins made were the best I have ever had from any bartender. Not to say I haven't had amazing cocktail experiences with other bartenders, I have for sure, but Erik's style was so clean and respectful to the ingredients. His understanding and balance of cocktails were so unique and different from almost anyone else. I soaked it all up and feel that my cocktails always have that thing I learned from Erik. I learned and honed my craft working for him. He became my mentor and friend. I still bother and annoy him with questions. My bar is unmistakably an Erik Adkins-influenced cocktail program with a Daniel Hyatt bar setting.

TALK A BIT ABOUT WORKING AT TWO PLACES WITH WILDLY DIFFERENT CONCEPTS: THE HISTORIC TOSCA CAFE AND ALAMO DRAFTHOUSE?

Tosca Cafe was about creating a cocktail menu that connected to the spirit and the history of Tosca Cafe, dating back to 1919, with April Bloomfield's Italian cuisine. I wanted to make sure I didn't get held down to just an Italian bar concept. But I did focus on amaro and more of a contemporary Italy. I wanted to stay fun and not too serious, bring back some old San Francisco bar mentality. I wanted to have it be a show at the bar. I embraced the old white Tosca coats and I came up with a system where whenever we had a House Cappuccino order we would yell it out extremely loud across the bar for the Cap station to make it. That bartender would yell back the order to let me know he got it. I would then yell another order and tell him a count of cappuccinos ordered all day. When we got an order for a Ramos Gin Fizz, we would build the cocktail in the tin and shake it, and then throw it to the next bartender to shake and then the next bartender to shake and back. We tried to keep it a *Bar Bar*, and not just another restaurant bar. We had shot combos and I created the Popko Daiquiri where you get a shot of Wild Turkey 101 Bourbon and a daiquiri at the back. It was quite the scene! One of the most amazing experiences of my life.

Alamo was insane. I had to create two different bar programs at the same time with completely different staff. The bar program in the back was run like a kitchen with an expeditor. Bear Vs Bull, Alamo's primary bar, was a sort of first version of California Gold—hot-climate, Baker-style cocktails, a fresh beer focus, boilermaker menu, vinyl records. Everything I love and want, except it was hidden in a movie theater with no light and the bar was built out before I could have much say in it. When we finally got into the space, I was pretty unhappy with it, but the bar was well received and did very well. I had to write a schedule every week with thirty bartenders that matched with the movies that were played. It was nuts!

· SCORCHED ROSE ·

SPIRT WORKS DISTILLERY

A recent creation by this Sebastopol distillery (other than hand sanitizer) is a robust bourbon, which is showcased in this floral and beautifully balanced cocktail.

GLASSWARE: Coupe

GARNISH: Dried rose petals

- 1½ oz. Spirit Works Bourbon
- ¼ oz. Yes Cocktail Co. Hibiscus Rose Syrup
- ¾ oz. Yes Cocktail Co. Orgeat Syrup
- 1 oz. fresh lemon juice
- 2 dashes King Floyd's Scorched Pear Bitters
- 2 dashes King Floyd's Ginger Bitters

1. Add all of the ingredients, except the bitters, to a cocktail shaker with ice, shake vigorously, and strain into a coupe.

2. Add the bitters and garnish with dried rose petals.

· S.B.C. ·

The Sebastopol distillery's take on a Boulevardier is a great way to try their sloe gin and yet another excellent answer for when somebody wants a Negroni—but not exactly a Negroni.

GLASSWARE: Rocks glass

GARNISH: Orange peel

- 1 oz. Spirit Works Sloe Gin
- 1 oz. Spirit Works Bourbon
- 1 oz. Campari
- 1 dash Angostura Orange Bitters

1. Combine all of the ingredients in a cocktail shaker with ice, shake vigorously, and strain into a rocks glass over large ice cubes.

2. Garnish with orange peel.

· CUCUMBER MINT GIMLET ·

HANSON OF SONOMA DISTILLERY

When it's a 95 degree summer day in Sonoma, what else could you want besides a crisp, refreshing gimlet from the local vodka distilling specialist? Well, maybe enjoying this cocktail while poolside would even make it better.

GLASSWARE: Coupe

GARNISH: Lime and mint

- 2 oz. Hanson Organic Cucumber Vodka
- ½ oz. fresh lime juice
- ½ oz. simple syrup
- 1 sprig of mint

1. Add all of the ingredients to a cocktail shaker with ice, shake vigorously, and strain into a chilled coupe.

2. Garnish with the lime and mint.

· TIME'S ARROW II ·

MIMINASHI

With Suntory and Star Trek's help, here's a terrific play on a Negroni/Boulevardier from what was downtown Napa's popular izakaya, pre-pandemic; unfortunately it is no longer.

"I often find that affixing a suitable name to a cocktail is a challenge," says Andrew Salazar. "I want the title to say a little something about the drink without it sounding corny, pretentious, or ham-handed. A tried and true method I like to implement is using a cultural reference. Our initial cocktail list had a lot of allusions to different anime series. Since the base spirit of this cocktail is Toki, a Japanese whisky by Suntory, which translates to 'time,' I knew that I wanted to work around that idea. Recently, at the suggestion of a friend and colleague, I've been watching episodes of *Star Trek: The Next Generation*. There's a fun two-part episode called 'Time's Arrow' that is set (drumroll). . .in 19th century San Francisco! Just a bit of fun trivia. This is the second iteration of this drink, hence Time's Arrow II."

GLASSWARE: Old Fashioned glass
GARNISH: Sesame and Citrus Candy (see page 299)
or expressed orange peel

- 1 oz. Sesame-Infused Suntory Toki Japanese Whisky
- 1 oz. Luxardo Bitter Bianco
- 1 oz. Carpano Bianco Vermouth
- 1 bar spoon Oleo Salis

1. Combine all of the ingredients in a mixing glass with ice, stir, and strain into an Old Fashioned glass over a large ice cube.

2. Garnish with Sesame and Citrus Candy or expressed orange peel.

SESAME-INFUSED TOKI: Add 1 cup toasted sesame seeds to a 750 ml bottle of Toki Whisky and let stand for a couple days before straining off the solids.

OLEO SALIS: In a bowl, combine the zest of 10 lemons and 10 oranges with ½ cup kosher salt. Massage the mixture together (Salazar recommends wearing a latex glove) for a minute or so and allow the salt to act on the peels overnight to extract the essential oils. In order to collect as much of the oils as possible, add 2 oz. of Toki Whisky to the mix. Stir thoroughly and strain off the resulting liquid. Be sure to press out as much as you can.

SESAME AND CITRUS CANDY

The expressed orange peel is a lovely garnish for this drink. But making this savory candy makes for an unforgettable garnish.

1. Measure out ½ cup sugar. Add a small coat of the sugar to a saucepan over medium-high heat and wait for it to begin melting. Slowly and incrementally add more sugar to the spots in the pan where the sugar is liquefying. Once about a third of the sugar has been introduced, the pace can be increased as you add more sugar and begin to stir with a wooden spoon or heat-resistant spatula.

2. After all of the sugar has been converted into caramel, add 3 tablespoons mixed toasted, and black sesame seeds; zest of 1 lemon; zest of 1 orange; and ⅛ teaspoon baking soda. Stir well to distribute ingredients and incorporate the baking soda.

3. Once fully combined, pour the mixture onto a sheet-lined sheet pan. Use an off-set spatula to spread the caramel in a thin layer across the sheet.

4. While still hot, sprinkle 1 teaspoon Maldon sea salt over the surface.

5. After the caramel has cooled for approximately 1 minute, use a sharp knife to score the firm, yet slightly tacky, caramel candy in the shapes that you like.

6. Wait for the caramel to set fully before snapping along the score marks. Crosshatching in a simple rectangular pattern will yield the most usable pieces.

· ODE TO KIPLING ·

MIMINASHI

I f you like pisco punch, you'll love the riff on it from the brilliant mind of cocktail maestro Andrew Salazar.

GLASSWARE: Coupe

GARNISH: Hibiscus tincture

- 1½ oz. Coconut Butter-Washed BarSol Quebranta Pisco
- ¾ oz. Small Hand Foods Passion Fruit Syrup
- ¾ oz. fresh lime juice
- Hibiscus Tincture, to taste

1. Combine all of the ingredients, except the tincture, in a cocktail shaker with ice, shake vigorously, and double strain into a coupe.

2. Add the tincture with a liquid dropper.

COCONUT BUTTER-WASHED PISCO: Add 14 oz. virgin coconut oil to a saucepan over medium heat. Once melted, combine the oil with 750 ml bottle of Quebranta Pisco, stir to combine, and let stand at room temperature overnight. After removing the fat cap, pass the pisco through a coffee filter to catch any small bits that may remain.

HIBISCUS TINCTURE: Fill a pint container to the top with dried hibiscus flowers and fill with BarSol Quebranta Pisco. Let stand overnight, strain, and store.

· MAI TAI ·

MIMINASHI

When a mai tai meets a margarita . . . That is sort of the premise for this drink, which omits sugar syrups for a more tart profile. You get the rum—Miminashi combined four kinds: Smith and Cross Navy Strength, Hampden Estate, Blackwell, and Trois Rivières Vieux Agricole—and orgeat of a mai tai, plus the tart-citrus components taken from a margarita formula. Two classics meet here in beautiful cocktail harmony.

GLASSWARE: Old Fashioned glass
GARNISH: Spent lime shell and sprig of mint

- 1½ oz. rum
- ¾ oz. fresh lime juice
- ½ oz. curacao
- ½ oz. orgeat

1. Combine all the ingredients with enough crushed ice to fill an Old Fashioned glass.

2. Pour the contents back and forth from the glass to the cocktail shaker a few times in order to chill and dilute.

3. Once properly mixed, garnish with half of a juiced lime, the result being a lime shell that has brought to the surface the essential oils in the rind.

4. Add the mint sprig next to the lime shell in the suggestion of a deserted island with a lone palm tree.

· NAVY GROG ·

MIMINASHI

This riff on an oft-forgotten early rum cocktail classic. is more in line with the Donn Beach version than the Trader Vic's one.

GLASSWARE: Old Fashioned glass
GARNISH: Lime wedge and sprig of mint

- 2 oz. bottled rum blend
- ½ oz. Demerara overproof rum
- ¾ oz. fresh lime juice
- ¾ oz. Oroblanco grapefruit juice
- ¾ oz. Honey-Ginger Mix
- Soda water, to top

1. Combine all of the ingredients, except the soda water, in a cocktail shaker with ice, shake vigorously, and strain into a glass over an ice cone (packed crushed ice).

2. Top with soda water, approximately ¾ oz., and garnish with lime wedge and mint. Use a chopstick to jam a hole through the ice cone for the straw to access the drink.

HONEY-GINGER MIX: Press fresh ginger for its juice and combine it with an equal amount, by volume, of honey. Stir thoroughly to combine.

GOOSE & GANDER

The sweet-umami sensation of candy cap mushrooms is the core of this Japanese whisky cocktail created by Goose & Gander's bar manager, Emma Kreis. Ultimately, it's just a three-ingredient cocktail, but in reality, there are a half dozen different elements at play that make for a dignified, multi-layered cocktail. And, I'm sure that the restaurant and bar workers reading this understand the inside joke of the cocktail's name—"86" is restaurant terminology for when an ingredient or a menu item runs out.

GLASSWARE: Nick & Nora glass

GARNISH: Lemon peel

- St. George Absinthe Verte, to rinse
- 1½ oz. Candy Cap Butter-Washed Suntory Toki Japanese Whisky
- 1 oz. Sarsaparilla Syrup
- 1 oz. fresh lemon juice

1. Rinse the Nick & Nora glass with the absinthe.

2. Combine the whisky, syrup, and lemon juice in a cocktail shaker with ice, hard shake for approximately 30 seconds, and double strain into the glass.

3. Garnish with a lemon peel.

CANDY CAP BUTTER-WASHED WHISKY: Add ½ lb. unsalted butter to a saucepan over medium heat. Cook until very slightly golden. Remove from heat and place in a large freezer-safe container. Add 1 (750 ml) bottle Suntory Toki Japanese Whisky to the butter, whisking constantly for about 2 minutes. Add 3 grams candy cap mushrooms, and stir to combine. Freeze overnight. Strain the whisky through a fine-mesh strainer lined with cheesecloth. Store the whisky in the refrigerator until ready to use.

SARSAPARILLA SYRUP: Add 8 oz. Indian sarsaparilla, cut and sifted, and 48 oz. water to a pot over medium-high heat and bring to a boil. Reduce by half and then strain through a mesh strainer. Add 24 oz. sugar and whisk thoroughly to combine. Store in the refrigerator until ready to use.

· BALI SPICE OLD-FASHIONED ·

GOOSE & GANDER

Many of the world's great cocktails were inspired by intrepid traveling bartenders. While Scott Beattie was traveling in Bali, Goose & Gander owner Andy Florsheim gave Beattie a call about opening the bar. Beattie came back to California with a giant stick of cinnamon and the idea for this take on an Old Fashioned using a trio of spices to give the bourbon drink a whole new savory dimension.

GLASSWARE: Rocks glass

GARNISH: Orange slice

- 2 oz. St. George Spirits Breaking & Entering Bourbon
- ¼ oz. Bali Spice Syrup
- 1 dash Regans' Orange Bitters
- 1 dash Bitter Truth Orange Bitters
- Zest of 1 orange

1. Add all of the ingredients, except the zest, to a mixing glass, add enough ice to fill the glass two-thirds of the way up, stir for 20 to 30 seconds to dilute, and strain into a rocks glass over 1 large ice cube.

2. Spray orange oil using a citrus zester over the top of the drink and garnish with a slice of orange.

BALI SPICE SYRUP: Break 9 inches of cinnamon sticks into small pieces. Add those pieces to a spice grinder, along with 12 cloves and 12 star anise pods. Grind until the spices become dust-like, about 1 minute. Add the ground spices to a saucepan over medium heat and toast them until slightly smoking and aromatic. Keep the pan moving constantly and be sure not to burn the spices. After about 2 minutes, add 16 oz. simple syrup. Bring to a boil; then lower heat and simmer for about 5 minutes. Turn off the heat and let the syrup cool, about 1 hour. After it is cooled, stir the bottom of the pan to get all the little spicy bits off the bottom and strain through a mesh strainer or chinois. It might take up to an hour to get all the liquid out, but you can force it through with a spatula for faster results.

· CUCUMBER COLLINS ·

SCOTT BEATTIE,
CREATED FOR GOOSE & GANDER

The Napa Valley is famous for its cabernet sauvignon—and its signature cocktail, Scott Beattie's Cucumber Collins. It is a year-round standard at Goose & Gander, and particularly beloved on the many 90 degree summer days in St. Helena. Along with the Chartreuse Swizzle, it's the Bay Area's other signature drink of the 21st century. Beattie's invention here touches on many modern themes: local ingredients, a photogenic drink, and resourceful use of ingredients (note how the huckleberries contribute to the pickled purple cucumbers).

GLASSWARE: Collins glass
GARNISH: Cucumbers and berries

- 1½ oz. Square One Cucumber Vodka
- ½ oz. fresh lemon juice
- ¼ oz. yuzu juice
- ½ oz. simple syrup
- 1½ oz. chilled soda water
- 5 thin English cucumber slices
- 5 thin Pickled Purple Cucumber slices
- 1 tablespoon Pickled Huckleberries

1. Add the vodka, juices, and syrup to the short half of a mixing tin. Fill to the top with ice and seal it up.

2. Shake just a few times to mix, then unseal, leaving everything in the larger half.

3. Add the chilled soda water to the mixture, swirl it around a few times to mix, and then dump everything into a 12 oz. Collins glass.

4. Garnish with the two kinds of cucumbers and the berries.

PICKLED HUCKLEBERRIES: Add 6 cups unseasoned rice vinegar, 2 cups mirin, and 2 cups cooking sake to a saucepan over medium-high heat and bring to a boil. When the liquid boils, add 3 cups granulated white sugar and stir to dissolve. Add 2 lbs. wild huckleberries and return to a boil. When the mixture reaches a boil, remove from heat and let cool. Strain off excess liquid and reserve for Pickled Purple Cucumber recipe. Refrigerate the the strained berries; they will last up to 1 month.

PICKLED PURPLE CUCUMBERS: Add ¾ qt. reserved Pickled Huckleberries pickling liquid and ¾ qt. thinly sliced English cucumbers to a large container, cover, and refrigerate for 24 hours. The color should set after 24 hours. The cucumbers will keep for 2 months in the refrigerator.

SCOTT BEATTIE

BEVERAGE DIRECTOR, MEADOWOOD EVENTS

I think that it's fair to say that Scott Beattie has influenced seasonal produce-driven cocktails by bartenders in the way that Alice Waters did for seasonal produce-driven cooking. Beattie's impact on the Bay Area bar scene—and way beyond—is impossible to quantify. "Scott Beattie was doing dehydrated citrus and all of that 15-16 years ago, long before you were seeing that as standard at every bar," says Virginia Miller (see page 64). "And it was just stuff from his backyard!"

Born in San Francisco, Beattie got the bartending/front-of-house bug and eventually moved north after the dot com bubble crash of the late 1990s. In St. Helena, he became part of a near-perfect cocktails dream team at Martini House: chef Todd Humphries's food and modern-speakeasy-luxury design by architect extraordinaire, and owner, Pat Kuleto. Being surrounded by the bountiful produce of the Napa Valley laid the groundwork for his job running the bar program at Cyrus in Healdsburg, at the time one of the most renowned high-end dining experiences in the country. In 2008, his book *Artisanal Cocktails* came out and today it is still considered the definitive seasonal cocktails book. Beattie returned to St. Helena to work at Goose & Gander, Martini House's replacement, and now he's taking his cocktail talents to the crowds—literally—by creating drinks for weddings, parties, and other big events for the luxurious Meadowood Napa Valley, tucked away off the Silverado Trail.

Overlooking Meadowood's 9-hole golf course and immaculate croquet lawn, we talked in spring 2020 about Beattie's cocktails philosophy and career. Sadly, at that time as the COVID-19 pandemic was just beginning, little did we know that 6 months later there would be the tragic Glass Fire affecting that magnificent Meadowood property and much of its surrounding area.

ON GETTING INTO THE INDUSTRY IN THE FIRST PLACE . . .

I just fell in love with the business. It was the first time in my life I actually had my pockets full. I didn't realize until I got into it that you could make so much money in tips (Double shift! Second job!) . . .I was just all over it. I just wanted to have money to take my girlfriend out and go see shows. It was the sense of empowerment as a young person and the city was affordable back then. My rent was $530 a month, which I split with my girlfriend.

IT WAS TOUGH TO CONVINCE DRINKERS TO ORDER SOMETHING DIFFERENT THAN THEIR GO-TO STANDARDS AT THE TIME (LATE 1990S) . . .

My dad had all these awesome citrus trees and I was like, alright, let's take some of this handmade Meyer lemon vodka that Marco of Charbay (referring to Charbay Distillery, one of our pioneering local spirits producers) makes, I'll mix it with Meyer lemon juice, and that's how I'm going to make my lemon drops. And I'm going to take this blood orange vodka, a little blood orange juice and start making Cosmos that way. It was taking the familiar things and make them using better ingredients, and also learning to back off on sugar.

WE OFTEN FORGET ABOUT HOW THE WINE CULTURE OF FINE DINING CHANGED MUCH EARLIER THAN COCKTAILS . . .

You had to have a comprehensive wine program with things from the old world and things from here. And that changed. But the bar part just remained the same. The 70s were not a good time to be drinking. If you think about it – Harvey Wallbangers, all those silly drinks, and people would just stick to those classic ones they liked.

BUT THE COCKTAIL WORLD FINALLY CAUGHT UP. YOUR PRO-GRAM AT GOOSE & GANDER EVEN HAD 50 COCKTAILS PLUS AN AMAZING ICE PROGRAM.
Our ice program was pretty ambitious. We would buy huge blocks of ice that I would bring up from San Francisco, chainsaw it in the back parking lot and hand-cut them. We would go through sometimes a hundred or more per night.

AND A WORD ON THAT WHOLE NEW YORK IS BETTER THAN SAN FRANCISCO DEBATE . . .
People were trying to Biggy and Tupac the whole situation for a while, like East Coast versus West Coast. The East Coast bar theory was more focused on really meticulous execution and lots of bottles. The west coast, at least in the San Francisco Bay Area, was more focused on seasonality and produce. What's in season? How do we process it? How can we do something that speaks to the time of year?

EAST BAY

THE VIRGIN'S SACRIFICE

BEE'S KNEES

BOTANIVORE GIN FIZZ

VAN CANDY

LAST TANGO

THE HARP

TOMATO BEEF

GOLDEN TRIANGLE

BOURBON & SPICE

THE TOUGH GET GOING

ONE WAY FLIGHT

CHARLOTTE'S WEB

SANGRÍA TELEFÈRIC

D irectly east of San Francisco on the other side of the Bay are Oakland and Berkeley, two major cities for very different reasons. Oakland is a diverse, vibrant city (tons of great restaurants and bars; lots of distinct neighborhoods), while Berkeley is a university town with extensive Bohemian/counter-culture history. Many residential communities surround the areas between the Bay and East Bay hills, then extend from the eastern side of the East Bay hills further toward the Central Valley. Walnut Creek and Livermore are two of the other major cities in the East Bay, both with impressive food and drink scenes (and wine tasting in Livermore).

· THE VIRGIN'S SACRIFICE ·

THE KON-TIKI

This terrific downtown Oakland tiki bar goes all out in terms of island décor and using great ingredients to revitalize the genre's classics, while also creating some new-school tiki libations. This is one of those, based on the celebrated Carter Beats the Devil cocktail that The Slanted Door Group's Erik Adkins created for Flora in Oakland (Flora is now Palmetto, owned by The Kon-Tiki's Christ Aivaliotis). As Christ Aivalitotis puts it, think of this as tropical and spicy "Agave Tiki."

GLASSWARE: Tiki mug

GARNISH: Cherry, pineapple wedge, an orchid,
and two pineapple leaves

- 1½ oz. blanco tequila
- ½ oz. espadin mezcal
- ¾ oz. fresh lime juice
- ¾ oz. pineapple gum syrup
- ¼ oz. passion fruit syrup
- 5 dashes Thai Chili Tincture

1. Combine all of the ingredients to a cocktail shaker with a few cubes of ice, flash shake, and strain into a tiki mug over crushed ice.

2. Garnish with a cherry picked to a pineapple wedge, an orchid, and two pineapple leaves.

THAI CHILI TINCTURE: Add bird's eye chilis to Wray & Nephew Overproof Rum and let stand for 2 weeks. Strain and store.

· BEE'S KNEES ·

ST. GEORGE SPIRITS

With St. George's wonderful Botanivore Gin, packed with 19 botanicals, the honey-centric, three-ingredient classic Bee's Knees buzzes to new heights. It's simplicity at its finest.

GLASSWARE: Coupe

GARNISH: Lemon twist

- 2 oz. St. George Botanivore Gin
- ¾ oz. honey syrup
- ¾ oz. fresh lemon juice

1. Combine all of the ingredients in a cocktail shaker with ice, shake vigorously, and strain into a chilled coupe.

2. Garnish with a lemon twist.

· BOTANIVORE GIN FIZZ ·

ST. GEORGE SPIRITS

Take the classic gin fizz to another frothy, botanical level with one of the Bay Area's finest gins, courtesy of Alameda's acclaimed distillery.

GLASSWARE: Collins glass

- **2 oz. St. George Botanivore Gin**
- **1 oz. fresh lemon juice**

- **¾ oz. simple syrup**
- **1 egg white**
- **1 oz. club soda**

1. Combine all of the ingredients, except the club soda, in a cocktail shaker and dry shake for about 10 seconds. Add 3 or 4 ice cubes, then shake again vigorously.

2. Add the club soda to a Collins glass, then double strain the contents of the shaker into the glass.

LOCAL DISTILLERIES TO KNOW

DISTILLERY 209 (SAN FRANCISCO)
With history going back to the late 19th century, the former Napa Valley-now-San Francisco distillery is world-renowned for its beautifully balanced, fragrant gins. Some of the most notable small-batch reserve gins from 209 are aged in wine barrels.

HMB DISTILLERY (HALF MOON BAY)
One of the Bay Area's smallest distilleries is located on the Peninsula's coastline, where husband-and-wife team Caesar and Ulli Bisono produce a small amount of high quality vodka and gin.

HANGAR ONE (ALAMEDA)
Vodka doesn't always have the greatest reputation. In the Bay Area, however, craft vodka is a big deal because of this East Bay distillery that continues to be one of the gold standards for vodka in the country—and pretty much the whole world. From fennel to mandarin blossoms, the vodkas are flavored with all kinds of fresh produce and spices. The vodka specialist also just released "Bentwing," its first brandy. For a quick history refresher, Hangar One was St. George's mega-successful vodka brand but is no longer affiliated with St. George after being sold in 2014. And, yes, Hangar One's home is an old aircraft hangar in the former Alameda Naval Air Station complex that is now a boomtown of breweries, wineries, and distilleries.

HOTALING & CO. (SAN FRANCISCO)
Fritz Maytag (the former owner of Anchor Brewing) started Anchor Distilling Company in 1993, as the spirits producing sibling of the famous Potrero Hill brewery. Anchor started off by producing three pot-distilled rye whiskeys (the only one doing so when it started in 1994) before unveiling the highly influential (and still beloved) Juni-

pero Gin. After Maytag sold the brewery in 2010, the distillery the distiller was renamed as Hotaling & Co. The company's portfolio now includes spirits produced from around the world.

LOCH & UNION (NAPA)
With stellar barley gin and American dry gin produced on custom-built copper stills from Germany, Napa's newest distillery is a standout in the entire Bay Area and rapidly becoming a favorite among top local bartenders.

NAPA VALLEY DISTILLERY (NAPA)
Wine isn't the only alcohol production show in town for Napa—this Napa producer continues to be a popular destination for locals and tourists hoping to sample some brandy, whiskey, or gin. There is both a tasting bar in the Oxbow Market and the "Grand Tasting Salon" at the distillery itself that the producer playfully describes as "One-part Art Deco Speakeasy, One-part Tiki Room and All-parts fun." It is indeed quite fun and a nice change-up from all the cabernet sauvignon tasting.

OAKLAND SPIRITS CO. (OAKLAND)
Uptown Oakland is one of the greatest neighborhoods for enjoying a cocktail in the Bay Area. The neighborhood also has its own excellent distillery for adding spirits to many of those cocktails or just sampling them neat at the tasting room (which shares space with two terrific wineries). It's the rare local distillery to make an amaro, but the core of its portfolio is comprised of uniquely flavored brandies and gins (shiso, oysters, seaweed).

RAFF DISTILLERIE (SAN FRANCISCO)
Previously located on Treasure Island, the beloved small distillery is now producing its Barbary Coast Rhum (Agricole), Emperor Norton Absinthe and Bummer & Lazarus Gin in the Bayview neighborhood of the city. Master Distiller Carter Raff is a fifth-generation San Franciscan

and his affection for the city's deep history shows in the spirits' name-sakes that nod to some of the quirkier characters of San Francisco's past.

RUSSELL CITY DISTILLERY (HAYWARD)

After founding one of the country's first brewpubs, Buffalo Bill's Brew-ery in Hayward, (East Bay) in the early 1980s, Geoff Harries expanded with this distillery in 2010. The RCD Vodka (made from "Yosemite's spring snowmelt") is their signature and more recently has been joined by small-batch rum, gin, and a Reposado agave spirit.

ST. GEORGE SPIRITS (ALAMEDA)

Think of St. George Spirits in the same *spirit* (pardon the pun) as Apple in terms of being a world-renowned pioneer from the Bay Area—and they even roughly came of age in the same time period. Jörg Rupf founded St. George in 1982 as the first small American distillery cre-ated since Prohibition and mainly focused on fruit brandies/eau de vies. Fast forward to 1996 when former nuclear scientist Lance Win-ters arrived and became Master Distiller, forming a dynamic tandem that led St. George to produce its first single malt whiskey and the Hangar One vodkas, setting the stage for substantial growth to where it is today as America's most influential distillery. Rupf retired in 2010, but the distillery continues to be in very good hands with Winters and Head Distiller Dave Smith. The portfolio has greatly expanded and is a virtual who's who of beloved spirits, from the California-themed Ter-roir Gin to the New Orleans coffee-style liqueur that has almost single-handedly made high-quality coffee cocktails possible for bartenders.

SEVEN STILLS (SAN FRANCISCO)

While you'll see a few brewery/distillery duos around the country, this young upstart is the only one around that combines both the spirits and beer production world. The distillery started in the Dogpatch in 2013 and soon opened a larger facility in the Bayview. Now it has an even grander home, complete with a restaurant and bar, in an industrial area at the edge of the Design District and Mission Bay. Whiskeys distilled from their own beer are the signature of Seven Stills (yes, named for San Francisco's seven hills!), but the distillery also produces excellent renditions of vodka, gin, barrel-aged gin, and pisco. Since we're first and foremost a cocktails book, I'd be remiss to not point out that the Mission Bar restaurant's cocktails are so good that you might stay for another round instead of catching the start of the game at the nearby Oracle Park or Chase Center. Two top San Francisco cocktail minds, Christopher Longoria (see more about his work at Che Fico in this book) and Nora Furst (True Laurel, California Gold), created the menu of three drinks for each of Seven Stills' five main spirits.

SPIRIT WORKS (SEBASTOPOL)
Sloe gin is still barely known by most Bay Area drinkers. Thanks to this Sonoma County distillery, the sloe berry-infused spirit with a long history in England is starting to have a higher profile locally. Appropriately for what is arguably its signature spirit, husband-and-wife owners Timo and Ashby Marshall like to playfully say sloe gin combines the British and California worlds just like their distillery (he's from England, Ashby is from the west coast). Spirit Works is located in the Barlow (along with Fern Bar as you'll later learn), a vast complex of restaurants, breweries, wineries, and artisans in Sebastopol. With that food & drink paradise backdrop, Spirit Works is one of the most frequently visited distilleries in the Bay Area. But, that's honestly also because they're producing some of the finest spirits in the country, which bartenders would gladly tell you. Spirit Works just released their first bourbon and boast a substantial amount of across-the-board great spirits, from vodka to straight rye whiskey.

STILLWATER SPIRITS (PETALUMA)
It's no secret that Petaluma (southern Sonoma County) is one of the food & drink centers of the Bay Area, from the many local dairies and breweries, to the upstart restaurants and wineries. There's also a great distillery on that roster of artisans, creating various styles of brandy,

grappa, vodka, whisky, and gin since 2004, when brewer Brendan Moylan (Marin Brewing Co. in Larkspur) founded it.

SUTHERLAND DISTILLING CO. (LIVERMORE)
Livermore has it all—great wine, great cocktails, great breweries—and there's also this terrific distillery started in 2013. Sutherland was the first distillery in California to produce a straight bourbon, and now has a relatively wide portfolio led by a very rare-to-find locally made Navy strength rum and silver rum.

TREECRAFT DISTILLERY (SAN FRANCISCO)
With Raff's move to the mainland, this five-year old distillery is now the lone spirits producer remaining on Treasure Island, along with a few wineries and a handful of restaurants. The island is a former Naval base in the middle of San Francisco Bay (at roughly the midpoint of the Bay Bridge) and Treecraft resides in the former Naval firehouse. Founders/distillers Nate Byerly and Gordon Rempel started distilling as a hobby in Rempel's Sonoma County tree house—and now several years later, they're producing some of the most unique spirits in the Bay Area, like lavender hibiscus gin, chocolate bourbon (using San Francisco's Dandelion Chocolate), and a stellar rum that really would be perfect for drinks on the island or either side of the Bay.

· VAN CANDY ·

HOTSY TOTSY CLUB

V ery few bars tie together the worlds of high-level cocktails and loveable neighborhood dive better than the Hotsy Totsy Club in Albany. If only every town could have a place like the Hotsy Totsy! Jessica Maria's smartly designed, unfussy cocktails fit right in with the atmosphere of music from a 45 rpm jukebox and the occasional yelp of victory from shuffleboard games. Everyone is relaxed. Everyone is having fun. It's hard to replicate a place that has been in business since 1939 and still does what it does better than pretty much anybody else.

GLASSWARE: Coupe

GARNISH: Good & Plenty Candy

- 1 oz. Dolin Blanc
- ½ oz. London Dry gin
- ½ oz. absinthe
- ½ oz. blue curacao

- ½ oz. fresh lemon juice
- ⅓ oz. Small Hands Foods Gum Syrup
- 1 strip of lemon peel

1. Combine all of the ingredients, except the lemon peel, in a cocktail shaker with ice, shake vigorously, and double strain into a coupe.

2. Rub the rim of the glass with oil from the lemon peel and toss. Garnish with a speared Good & Plenty.

EAST BAY LOCALS' SPOTS

"A Garbage Bar for Losers": that's a great, albeit quite sarcastic, introduction from Eli's Mile High, a favorite Oakland watering hole. It's one
of the many noteworthy East Bar bars that are full of personality, awesome fun, and good (oftentimes terrific) drinks. These are golden bars
for winners in reality. Heinold's First and Last Chance Saloon in Jack
London Square opened in 1884 and will make you squint, questioning
reality before even having a drink, as it looks like it literally was
dropped from another planet and century into present-day Oakland.
Forbidden Island in Alameda is often considered the Bay Area's premier classic tiki bar; the Fat Lady's Victorian architecture is magnificent; and the White Horse is one of the oldest gay bars still operating
today. UC Berkeley students share billiards and trivia night with craft
beer nerds at the venerable Albatross; and cocktail nerds and Fox
Theatergoers alike enjoy the famous greyhounds with puckery fresh
grapefruit juice at Cafe Van Kleef. And, the "Oakland" wall graffiti of
the beer garden at craft beer favorite Lost & Found is one of the East
Bay's selling points that it just might be friendlier and more fun east of
Treasure Island.

Cafe Van Kleef

Eli's Mile High

The Fat Lady

Forbidden Island

Heinold's

Hotsy Totsy

King Fish

Lost & Found

White Horse Inn

· LAST TANGO ·

FLORA

Flora seems to have a lot of cross-pollination when it comes to its influence on Oakland's cocktail scene. It was the inspiration for The Virgin's Sacrifice (see page 320) and here it is again, as this was the first cocktail that Kimberly Rosselle put on the menu when she worked at the now-closed Uptown Oakland destination. Since then, Rosselle worked with the Bon Vivants as one of the lead bartenders for Trick Dog and Bon Voyage! Now, her cocktail designs can be found a few blocks away from where Flora was. Rosselle is the bar consultant for Oakland's new Friends and Family, one of the few all-female hospitality management teams in the Bay Area.

GLASSWARE: Coupe

GARNISH: Lime peel

- 1½ oz. Bombay Dry Gin
- 1 oz. St. Germain Elderflower Liqueur
- ¾ oz. fresh lime juice
- 5 Luxardo cherries
- 8-10 drops Bird's Eye Chili Tincture

1. Combine all of the ingredients in a cocktail shaker and muddle the cherries. Add cubed ice, shake vigorously, and double strain into a chilled coupe.

2. Garnish with a lime peel.

BIRD'S EYE CHILI TINCTURE: In a mason jar, combine 25 g dried bird's eye chili and 2 ½ oz. overproof rum. Infuse for 24 hours, strain, and store.

· THE HARP ·

FRIENDS AND FAMILY

Kimberly Rosselle's take on a martini heads in an herbal, bright and smooth direction, thanks to the additions of pine, sage, tarragon and Manzanilla sherry. You can almost hear the wind in the forest and taste the distinctly Northern California mix of herbs just by reading the recipe. As for the cocktail's namesake, Rosselle explains: "Named after Shelly Harper, a dear friend, and also the artist responsible for the Friends and Family sign hanging above the bar entrance and the specialty cocktail picks."

GLASSWARE: Cocktail glass

GARNISH: Olives

- 1¾ oz. Infused Tanqueray 10 Gin
- ¾ oz. Dolin Dry
- ¼ oz. Hidalgo Manzanilla Sherry
- 1 bar spoon olive brine

1. Combine all of the ingredients in a mixing glass with ice, stir, and strain into a chilled cocktail glass.

2. Garnish with 3 olives on a pick.

INFUSED GIN: Add 25 grams fresh pine, 5 grams fresh sage, 5 grams tarragon, and 5 whole bay leaves to 500 ml Tanqueray 10 Gin and let stand for 13 hours. Strain and store.

· TOMATO BEEF ·

VIRIDIAN

In early 2020, just before the COVID-19 pandemic struck the Bay Area, Viridian opened in Uptown Oakland with a giant wave of excitement. It's the rare high-energy/high-volume/high-quality cocktails establishment that is an effortlessly hip Hong Kong and 90s R&B scene

The cocktail program is orchestrated by bar manager and Oakland native William Tsui (previously at Lazy Bear and Rich Table), who manages to make abstract ideas seem fully functional and drinkable in cocktail form, without the superfluous gaudy elements that many modern drinks tend to have. The cocktails are mesmerizing in terms of their flavor and purity—I've never had such a vivid *guava* guava-centered drink before Viridian.

I wanted to make sure the Tomato Beef was part of this collection since it's easily one of the finest drinks I had in 2020. The profile is tangy, umami, and like a pristine plate of tomato-burrata-basil caprese on a beautiful patio in August.

GLASSWARE: Rocks glass
GARNISH: Pink peppercorn sprig

- 1¼ oz. blanco tequila
- ¼ oz. basil eau de vie
- 1 oz. Tomato Water

- ½ oz. Pink Peppercorn Syrup
- ½ oz. fresh lime juice*

1. Combine all of the ingredients in a mixing glass with ice, stir until cold, and strain into rocks glass over ice.

2. Garnish with pink peppercorn sprig.

TOMATO WATER: Blend tomatoes and strain through a coffee filter.

PINK PEPPERCORN SYRUP: Add 750 grams sugar and 500 ml water to a saucepan over medium-high heat to make 1 liter of simple syrup (or use the ratio of 1 ½ parts white cane sugar to 1 part water). Add 10 sprigs pink peppercorn leaf or 2 tablespoons pink peppercorns to the syrup, simmer for about 20 minutes, strain, and store.

At the bar, William Tsui uses a mixture of acids to create "not lime." For the home bartender fresh lime juice works, but the cocktail will no longer have the same clarity.

VIRIDIAN

The Golden Triangle is another great vegetable-centric creation from this immensely enjoyable Uptown Oakland bar. This is a particularly elegant, beautifully composed cocktail with a gentle earthy beet note in the background.

GLASSWARE: Martini glass

GARNISH: Beet chip or gold flake

- 1 ¼ oz. London dry gin
- 1 oz. LN Mattei Cap Corse
- ¾ oz. Grand Poppy Amaro
- ¼ oz. Suze
- 1 bar spoon Yellow Beet Syrup

1. Combine all of the ingredients in a mixing glass with ice, stir until cold, and strain into a martini glass.

2. Garnish with a beet chip or a little gold flake.

YELLOW BEET SYRUP: Clean and slice yellow beets. Add beets and simple syrup (1 ½ parts white cane sugar to 1 part water) to a saucepan over medium-high heat. Simmer the beets until tender. Strain and store.

· BOURBON & SPICE ·

BARDO LOUNGE & SUPPER CLUB

The glitzy mid-20th century supper club meets 21st century cocktail culture at this friendly, sleek hotspot in Oakland's Grand Lake district. Here's an autumnal leaning stirred bourbon cocktail from bar manager Brice Sanchez. Here's how assistant general manager Shannon Richey explains the drink: "Originally concocted as part of our seasonal cocktail menu, it's essentially a wintery take on a classic Old Fashioned. With the addition of sweet, herbaceous Montenegro, and spiced pear liqueur from St. George, one of our favorite local distilleries, the Bourbon & Spice is everything nice. Finished with housemade fire bitters, which have been infused with mulling spices and chilis, this drink will keep you warm all winter long."

GLASSWARE: Rocks glass
GARNISH: Orange peel

- 1 oz. Bulleit Bourbon
- ½ oz. Amaro Montenegro
- ½ oz. St. George Spiced Pear Liqueur
- 1 dash Regan's Orange Bitters
- 1 dash Hellfire Habanero Bitters
- ½ bar spoon rich brown sugar (2:1 ratio brown sugar to water)

1. Combine all of the ingredients in a mixing glass with ice, stir, and strain into a rocks glass over a big cube.

2. Garnish with an expressed orange peel.

JUANITA & MAUDE

The quiet city of Albany, Berkeley's neighbor to the north, is home to this ideal farm-to-table, friendly neighborhood/special occasion spot from chef/owner Scott Eastman and owner/designer Ariane Owens. General manager/bar and wine director Nicholas Danielson is the talented mind behind the noteworthy cocktail menu with many consistent highlights like this take on the East Bay's own classic, the mai tai.

GLASSWARE: Large tumbler

GLASSWARE: Orange peel

- 1½ oz. Royal Standard Rum
- ½ oz. fresh orange juice
- ½ oz. orgeat
- ½ oz. Pierre Ferrand
- ¼ oz. fresh lime juice
- ½ oz. 12-Year-Old Ron Abuelo Dark Rum

1. Combine all of the ingredients, except the dark rum, in a cocktail shaker with ice, shake vigorously, and strain into a large tumbler over ice.

2. Float dark rum on top and garnish with a wide strip of orange peel.

SOBRE MESA
SUSAN EGGETT

This downtown Oakland cocktail destination looks to the Caribbean and Latin America for inspiration. Susan Eggett is a consultant for the bar and designed this Brazil-by-way-of-Sonoma stirred cocktail with partial notes of a Manhattan: "This drink was inspired by a traditional Brazilian cocktail called Rabo de Galo. That translates to 'tail of the rooster' aka cocktail! Two of my rum regulars brought this drink to my attention after a trip they took to Brazil and I fell in love with it. We are hoping our version, which we adapted for Sobre Mesa, can fill the need/trend we are seeing in the rum world for spirit-forward rum drinks. We also hope this drink will excite traditional Manhattan drinkers. For the base, we are using a 45% abv rye whiskey called Redwood Empire that is aged and bottled in Sonoma. The cachaça then becomes a modifier in our version. The Avua Amburana brings a warm element of cinnamon and other baking spices, which balances beautifully with the rye. The richness of Pedro Ximenez Sherry and a new aperitivo style Nonino round out the drink in a subtle way that we hope can surprise and delight our guests. Layers of flavor that taste like they were meant for each other."

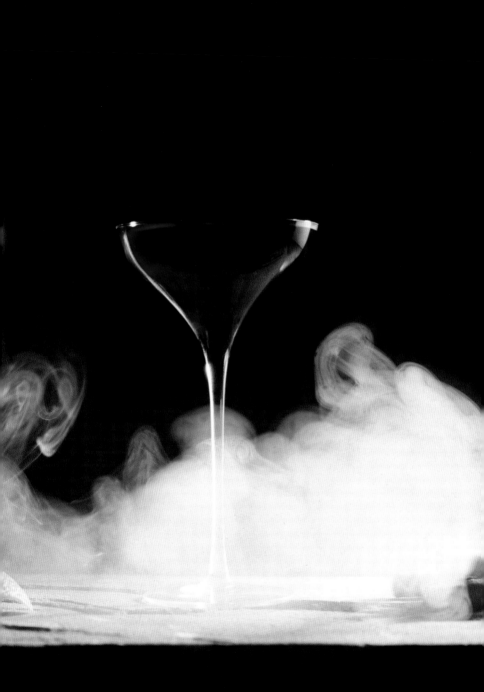

GLASSWARE: Coupe

GARNISH: Flamed orange peel

- 1½ oz. Redwood Empire Rye
- ½ oz. Avua Cachaça Amburana
- ½ oz. L'Aperitivo Nonino
- ½ oz. Aurora Pedro Ximenez Sherry
- 2 dashes Angostura Bitters

1. Combine all of the ingredients in a mixing glass with ice, stir, and strain into a coupe.

2. Garnish with a flamed orange peel.

RANGE LIFE

Livermore, located right where the East Bay meets the South Bay, has always been known for its wine country, but wasn't really a notable city for restaurants. Until two years ago, when two couples with strong restaurant experience pedigrees decided to open a restaurant together. Whether it's for Bill Niles's cooking, Sarah Niles's wine list featuring Livermore Valley wines and wines from way beyond, or the cocktails by Waine Longwell, Range Life is about as fine-tuned and polished of a casual restaurant as I've found in the Bay Area. Per Range Life's creative director Lauren Heanes-Longwell, this cocktail created by her husband actually has nothing to do with the E.B. White children's book that we all know and love: "This cocktail is named after the former horror-punk themed head shop that once inhabited Range Life's brick building. The resulting sour is nearly as smoky and spooky looking."

GLASSWARE: Coupe
GARNISH: Dehydrated pink grapefruit wheel and grated black lime

- 1½ oz. mezcal
- ½ oz. falernum
- ¾ oz. grapefruit juice
- ½ oz. fresh lime juice
- 1 egg white

1. Combine all of the ingredients in a cocktail shaker and dry shake. Add ice, shake again, and strain into a chilled coupe.

2. Garnish with the dehydrated grapefruit and grated black lime, to taste.

· SANGRÍA TELEFÈRIC ·

TELEFÈRIC BARCELONA

Nobody will confuse the two upscale Bay Area suburbs of Walnut Creek and Palo Alto with the beach life and Gaudi architecture of Barcelona, the city that Telefèric expanded to the Bay Area from. A big goblet of sangria and some modern tapas at this pair of chic restaurants will definitely help in transporting you to El Raval. And, don't be shy with an elaborate garnish.

GLASSWARE: Wine glass
GARNISH: Strawberries, berries, orange,
lemon, cinnamon, and mint

- 1 (750 ml) bottle Tempranillo
- 4 oz. brandy
- 4 oz. apple juice
- 4 oz. orange juice
- 4 oz. peach juice

1. Combine all of the ingredients in a mixing glass with ice, stir, and strain into a wine glass over ice.

2. Garnish with strawberries, berries, orange, lemon, cinnamon, and mint.

SOUTH BAY

HURRICANE

SHURA NO HANA

VESPER

BACK IN BLACK

BARN BURNER

THE DAVID

THE MARIO

THE MOJITO

The South Bay includes the vast sprawl of San Jose deep into the Santa Clara Valley, eventually reaching the Garlic Capital of the World, Gilroy. West and northwest of San Jose are the beautiful Santa Cruz Mountains, which turn into the Coastal Range running all the way north toward San Francisco. Nestled between these mountains and the Bay is Silicon Valley, the birthplace of computers and home to countless tech companies and Stanford University in Palo Alto. The area between Silicon Valley and San Francisco is often referred to as "The Peninsula," even though San Francisco is the tip of that peninsula and nobody ever refers to it as part of "the Peninsula." It's a quirk that I've never understood (and I grew up on the Peninsula). West of the Coastal Range, you'll find stunning (and very cold) beaches in towns like Half Moon Bay, with great surfing, some terrific restaurants—and, of course, unbeatable sunsets. Much of the West Coast's great seafood comes from the Pacific waters off the Peninsula (and back during Prohibition, contraband booze often arrived into this area).

· HURRICANE ·

THE BYWATER

T he worst cocktail I've ever had in my life was a Hurricane on Bourbon Street (I'll refrain from saying which bar), and that assured me that I will never have a Hurricane again in my life—at least until Manresa's David Kinch opened an ode to New Orleans in Los Gatos. That *laissez les bon temps roulé-*, beads-, and jambalaya-filled restaurant is The Bywater, the Bay Area's premier place to try all things NOLA-related. That includes the Hurricane cocktail for all those who were skeptical that it could become a bonafide excellent drink. The Bywater's version wiped away all my memories of that Bourbon Street moment.

GLASSWARE: Hurricane glass

GARNISH: Lemon

- 2 oz. Jamaican Rum Blend
- 1¼ oz. Passion Fruit Blend
- ¼ oz. fresh lemon juice
- 1 dash Peychaud's Bitters

1. Combine all of the ingredients in a cocktail shaker with crushed ice, whip shake for 3 times longer than usual, and dump the contents into the glass.

JAMAICAN RUM BLEND: Combine equal parts Hamilton Black Rum and Appleton Estate Rum and mix well.

PASSION FRUIT BLEND: In a large mason jar, combine 1 jar Perfect Purée Passion Fruit, 900 grams cane sugar, and 360 grams Campari and mix well.

· SHURA NO HANA ·

PAPER PLANE

The Bay Area needs to pay more attention to the San Jose cocktail scene. There might not be the sheer number of excellent bars that Oakland and San Francisco can boast of, but the great ones, like Paper Plane, are standouts for our entire metro region. This extremely unique gin-shiso-watermelon cocktail, designed by bar manager Ryan Ota and co-owner George Laulouh, is a terrific example of the creative edginess you'll find at their bar in the heart of downtown San Jose. While you're at Paper Plane, make sure to pause and take a look at the stunning bar backdrop, one of the most giant back bars I've ever seen.

"The cocktail is a reference to a 1973 Japanese song by Meiko Kaji, and it means "the flower of carnage." The song might sound familiar because it's played in *Kill Bill*. Most likely where you might have heard of it!" declares George Lahlouh.

GLASSWARE: Coupe
GARNISH: Shiso leaf

- 1½ oz. Roku Gin
- ¼ oz. Sidetrack Shiso Liqueur
- 2 oz. Watermelon Syrup
- ½ oz. fresh lemon juice
- 3 dashes Galangal Tincture

1. Combine all of the ingredients in a cocktail shaker with ice, shake vigorously, and strain into a chilled coupe glass.

2. Float a fresh shiso leaf to garnish.

WATERMELON SYRUP: Juice a seedless watermelon. Using a 3:1 ratio of juice to white sugar, combine juice and sugar in a container and stir vigorously. There shouldn't be any solid sugar granules left on the bottom of the container. After mixing thoroughly, strain through a chinois and store. It can be refrigerated for 7 to 10 days.

GALANGAL TINCTURE: Add 1 (750 ml) bottle Everclear, 300 grams fresh chopped galangal, and 34 grams dried galangal to a blender and blend thoroughly. Add the mixture to a 1-gallon sealable bag, making sure to remove as much air as possible. Cook the bag in a sous vide machine at 130 for 3 hours. After cooking, strain through a chinois, and then squeeze through a cheesecloth to remove all particulates. This will keep indefinitely in a glass jar stored at room temperature.

· VESPER ·

The Peninsula's most noteworthy 2019 opening was this timeless, deluxe stunner from the Bacchus Management Group. Classic cocktails (like the aforementioned martini) run the bar show here, which is fitting for the modern-elegant atmosphere and throwback American Continental cuisine given a contemporary revamp.

GLASSWARE: Cocktail glass

GARNISH: Lemon twist

- 1 dash Angostura Bitters
- 3 oz. frozen gin
- 1 oz. frozen vodka
- ½ oz. chilled Lillet Blanc

1. Add bitters to a chilled cocktail glass, swirl to coat.

2. Add the gin, vodka, and Lillet Blanc directly into the glass.

3. Garnish with a lemon twist.

THE LEXINGTON HOUSE

Los Gatos' The Lexington House toes the murky line between being a relaxed fine-dining restaurant and a refined cocktail bar as well as anyone does in the Bay Area. It's both harmoniously, as essentially one space—not the bar over here and the restaurant over there, and both with separate vibes. The Lexington House seamlessly bridges the best of both those worlds. No wonder then that it has been one of the South Bay's gold standards for dinner and cocktails since opening in 2013.

GLASSWARE: Any stem glass

- 1½ oz. Larceny Bourbon (or other quality favorite bourbon)
- ¾ oz. Fernet Vallet
- ¼ oz. Giffard Crème de Mure
- ½ oz. fresh lime juice
- ¼ oz. Black Pepper "Shrub"

1. Combine all of the ingredients in a cocktail shaker with ice, shake vigorously, and strain into chosen glassware.

BLACK PEPPER "SHRUB": Add 1 tablespoon black peppercorns to a saucepan over medium-high heat, and then add ¾ cup water and ¼ cup cider vinegar, followed by 1 cup raw sugar. Stir and keep over heat until fish eyes form. Remove from heat and let cool overnight at room temperature. Strain and store.

· BARN BURNER ·

THE LEXINGTON HOUSE

Mezcal's aggressive smoke is tamed by chocolate elements and prominent orange/herbal notes of a darker, richer amaro in one of The Lexington House's most beloved cocktails. Note that you can use pretty much any favorite bourbon and mezcal for the recipe.

GLASSWARE: Old Fashioned glass

GARNISH: Orange twist

- 1 ¼ oz. Rayu Mezcal
- ½ oz. Buffalo Trace Bourbon
- ½ oz. Paolucci Amaro (or similar, such as Averna or Lucano)
- ½ oz. Giffard Crème de Cacao
- 3 dashes Workhorse Rye Salted Cacao Bitters

1. Combine all of the ingredients in a mixing glass with ice, stir, and strain into an Old Fashioned glass with a large ice cube.

2. Express the orange twist and then discard it.

· THE DAV!D ·

MANRESA

One of the best kept secrets in all of the Bay Area cocktail world is that Manresa in Los Gatos has a short, outstanding bites and cocktails menu at its bar. Of course, in the dining room, it's all about the elaborate tasting menu, which just so happens to be one of the world's finest dining experiences currently thanks to chef/owner David Kinch and his team. That same approach carries over to the four-seat bar's bites and sips. Maybe it's the steep price barrier for entry for a drink and a small plate that keeps it a bit under-the-radar, or just the fact that being at the bar of a special occasion temple of gastronomy isn't typical. But, hey, it's hard to match the splendid cocktails and food served at this little bar.

David Kinch is indeed the "David" in this wonderfully built cocktail based on a hopped whiskey by the Northern California distillery Charbay. Nobody says that the best restaurants in the world have to serve the most avant-garde, impossible-to-understand cocktails. They just need to emphatically highlight the greatest ingredients, techniques, and flavor profiles, which is the case here.

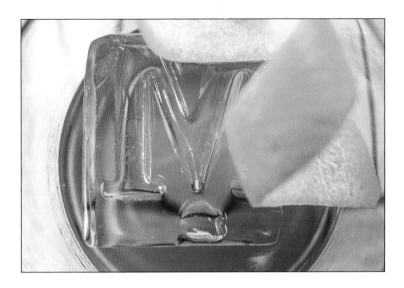

GLASSWARE: Large rocks glass

GARNISH: Orange peel

- 1½ oz. Charbay R5 Hopped Whiskey
- ¾ oz. Aperol
- ¾ oz. Carpano Antica Vermouth
- Splash of fresh squeezed Cara Cara orange juice

1. In a large rocks glass, add the ingredients over a large ice cube and stir gently to combine and lightly chill.

2. Express the oils from a large piece of orange peel over the top of the drink, wiping the oils on the rim of the glass before dropping it into the drink.

LA BODEGUITA DEL MEDIO

The Hemingway cocktail is a riff on a classic daiquiri, adding grapefruit and Maraschino liqueur to the formula. So, what is a riff of a riff? In that case, it has to be off-menu and come with a cigars-and-tobogganing story told by Michael Ekwall, the owner of La Bodeguita del Medio in Palo Alto.

"This is an off-menu, top-secret, *in the know*, cocktail which is my favorite of all our cocktails. It is named for Mario da Como (now retired) the barman that oversaw the Renaissance Bar at Badrutt's Palace in Saint Moritz, Switzerland. I was celebrating a birthday in Celerina, (in the Engadine Valley of Switzerland) with my wife Lara and a close friend, Michael Stevenson. Michael had joined us to participate (with me since women are not allowed) at an amateurs' day on the Cresta Run at the Saint Moritz Toboggan Club.

After a grueling day of tobogganing, we decided to celebrate my birthday with a cocktail and a cigar at Mario's bar. We ordered a couple of ice-cold daiquiris to enjoy with a cigar while watching a polo match on the frozen lake below. Mario obliged our order but suggested that he make us something 'just a little better.' How do you refuse such an offer? A few minutes later, he delivered us what is now our most famous 'secret cocktail' at La Bodeguita. Mario prepared our cocktails with Havana Club 3 Year, Havana Club 7 Year, Maraschino, fresh lime juice, fresh grapefruit juice, and a dash of bar sugar, all combined in a cocktail shaker and shaken, as Mario stated, 'until your hands begin to freeze', and then carefully poured into a waiting cocktail coupe."

GLASSWARE: Coupe

GARNISH: Sugar rim, optional

- 1 oz. Bacardi Limon Citrus Rum
- 1 oz. Plantation 5 Year Barbados Rum
- ¼ oz. Luxardo Maraschino liqueur
- ½ oz. fresh lemon juice
- ½ oz. fresh lime juice
- ½ oz. fresh ruby red grapefruit juice
- ½ teaspoon bar sugar

1. Fill a cocktail shaker with ice cubes, then add all of the ingredients. Shake hard, "ice cold hands hard."

2. Strain into a chilled cocktail coupe with an optional sugared rim.

· THE MOJITO ·

LA BODEGUITA DEL MEDIO

P alo Alto, my beloved hometown, is much more than just the home of tech companies and a major university, contrary to what much of the world thinks. Case in point: the city's two favorite bars. One is Antonio's Nut House, a dive bar with a caged gorilla holding free peanuts (definitely not included in this book's recipe section for reasons you can guess); the other is this Cuban-inspired rum bar that is constantly packed with longtime regulars, Stanford students on dates, and workers from the nearby offices. We're a long way at this La Bodeguita del Medio from its namesake in Havana, but after two Mojitos, those Teslas parked outside and self-driving cars rolling by start resembling the mid-century classic cars seen around the Cuban capital. Where do you start at La Bodeguita? Of course, the muddled mint cocktail that is made usually over a hundred times a day at the bar. One catch— don't forget the lemon juice. It's a curveball in the recipe that cannot be overlooked.

GLASSWARE: Collins glass

- ½ teaspoon bar sugar
- about 12 clean mint leaves (leave a little stem since they hold a bit of oil as well)
- 1½ oz. Bacardi Limon Citrus Rum
- ¼ oz. freshly squeezed lemon juice
- ¼ oz. freshly squeezed lime juice
- 3 oz. sparkling water

1. Add the mint to a tall Collins glass and sprinkle with sugar. Muddle the mint to extract the oils.

2. Add the rum and stir with the muddler. Add the juices and stir again. Add the sparkling water.

3. Add crushed ice. If you can find one, add a straw (paper-biodegradable), as it completes the experience.

APPENDIX

DANIEL HYATT TRIBUTE

VIRGINIA MILLER

Daniel Hyatt was the bar manager for the Alembic on Haight Street from 2007 to 2013, inspiring scores of bartenders to pursue cocktails as a profession and opening the eyes of countless guests to the world of quality cocktails and cocktail history. I know that I was one of those guests impacted greatly by Hyatt's influential work at the Alembic. But very few people knew the legendary bartender better than his friend and my fellow writing peer, Virginia Miller. So, I asked her to reflect on this great man who we lost way too soon.

"Hey, little buddy," Daniel Hyatt would greet me. As a hard-working oldest of four, who moved across the country solo from New Jersey to California at age 18, I'm "the strong, responsible one," not anyone's "little buddy." But Daniel *saw* me. He was that big brother many of us were never blessed to have. Maybe it was his crusty exterior, gruff voice, his claim to be "an old man by the time he was five." But he clearly knew what it was like to harbor a tender heart beneath a strong exterior.

Hyatt's tender generosity to all was his trademark. Pioneering bars and cocktails, his genius. He ran an ahead-of-its-time bar at the restaurant Winterland, shuttered in 2006. That same year, he launched the bar at Dave McLean's Alembic, making the small, Haight-Ashbury neighborhood bar home to the biggest American whiskey selection on the West Coast at the time.

He was one of the first outside the South to revive a proper Mint Julep and Vieux Carré, leading the Old Fashioned renaissance before the cocktail became ubiquitous. In those early days, Daniel would throw weekly Savoy Cocktail nights with Erik Ellestad (a San Francisco local who made every recipe in the classic London bar book via his Savoy Stomp blog.) Daniel had an early run on Pappy (the original Stitzel-Weller stuff) and other eventually-allocated whiskeys, being one of the few in the country regularly stocking it back then. He launched many great bartenders at Alembic, including Danny Louie (of Mister Jiu's) and chef-turned-bartender Larry Piaskowy (see page 205).

Hyatt's own cocktails walked that fine line of inventive and quaffable, with his trademark ease and dry humor. The past 15 years, his Southern Exposure—a vegetal-green beauty of gin, celery, lime— became legendary, published in cocktail recipe books, alongside drinks like Promissory Note (reposado tequila, dry vermouth, ginger liqueur, honey, absinthe, radish-lime-cinnamon garnish).

When Hyatt asked if I wanted a weekly bartending shift at The Alembic, I couldn't say no for the "behind the scenes" education alone. As a dining and drink writer (professionally since 2007 but studying it for years before), I'd been covering the cocktail renaissance as it unfolded, including pioneers like Hyatt. That weekly Wednesday shift was a gift I will cherish forever. The two of us made drinks, served regulars and industry friends, while talking for hours about our shared love of travel, literature, food, and, especially, music. We'd select playlists with care, digging deep into everything from classic country to jazz (oh, did he love Gram Parsons).

Daniel cared for each customer with that same self-effacing, affable gruffness, exuding a relaxed welcome to all. Sometimes he'd send me home with "a little something for you and your husband to enjoy," like a rare bottle of Cantillon beer or Idiazabel cheese from Spain. Hyatt was both a humble ground-breaker and a stellar human being.

I saw him two weeks before he died in May 2018. He gave me a big bear hug, introducing me as a "dear friend" to his work colleagues at 25 Lusk. We planned a record listening night two weeks out. He texted me after about how happy he was to see "my little buddy." I will forever regret not having that record night. So I play tunes, raise a cocktail, and toast one of the greatest barmen—and people—we'll ever know.

NEIGHBORHOOD GUIDES

With well over a hundred great destinations for cocktails—restaurants of all cuisines and price points, dives, snazzy cocktail hotspots, world-renowned cocktail bar classics—I couldn't include a recipe from *every* great bar. So, here's a handy list for the definitive bars all over the Bay Area. There will be a terrific cocktail at every one of these places. As Bay Area TV legend/Men's Wearhouse founder George Zimmer always says: "I guarantee it."

MISSION/DOGPATCH/POTRERO HILL/BERNAL HEIGHTS

ABV/Overproof
The Beehive
Beretta
Besharam
Bon Voyage!
Casements
Dear Inga
Elda
Elixir
El Techo
Foreign Cinema/Laszlo
Hawker Fare/Holy Mountain
Hideout at Dalva

Holy Water
Junior
Lazy Bear
Lolo
Lone Palm
Mochica
Piccino
The Sea Star
Third Rail
Trick Dog
True Laurel
Wildhawk
Zeitgeist (Bloody Mary)

Downtown/SoMa/Design District

83 Proof
Alchemist Bar & Lounge
Bellota
The Brixton on 2nd
The Cavalier
Hawthorn
The House of Shields
International Smoke
Local Edition
Marlowe
Michael Mina
Mourad
Natoma Cabana
Novela
Pabu
Perbacco
Rickhouse
ROOH
Saison
Seven Stills Brewery & Distillery
Tadich Grill
Tequila Mockingbird
Terminus
Trailblazer Tavern
The Treasury
The Vault

North Beach/Chinatown/Embarcadero

15 Romolo
Angler
Bix
Boulevard
Comstock Saloon
Cotogna
Gozu
Hard Water
Hog Island Oyster Co.
La Mar Cebicheria Peruana
Li Po Cocktail Lounge
Mister Jiu's
Moongate Lounge
Night Market
Original Joe's
Park Tavern
Prospect
Quince
The Slanted Door
Tony Nik's
Tosca Cafe

UNION SQUARE/NOB HILL/RUSSIAN HILL/TENDERLOIN/ HAYES VALLEY/CASTRO

1760
54 Mint
620 Jones
a Mano
Absinthe Brasserie & Bar
Anina
Bar 821
Benjamin Cooper
The Big Four
Blackbird
Bourbon & Branch
Brass Tacks
Charmaine's/Villon
Churchill
Last Rites

Liholiho Yacht Club/Louie's
  Gen-Gen Room
Macondray
Madrone Art Bar
Nightbird/ The Linden Room
Pacific Cocktail Haven
Peacekeeper
Pläj
Rich Table
Rye
Smuggler's Cove
Stookey's Club Moderne
Tonga Room
Whitechapel
Zombie Village

THE AVENUES/ HAIGHT/ NoPa/ PACIFIC HEIGHTS/ COW HOLLOW/ MARINA/ PRESIDIO

The Alembic
Anina
Aub Zam Zam
Aziza
Balboa Cafe
The Brixton
The Buena Vista
Che Fico
The Dorian

Finnegans Wake (Bloody Mary)
Flores
Horsefeather
The Interval at Long Now
Lost and Found
Maven
Monsieur Benjamin
Nopa
Nopalito

Outerlands
Padrecito
Palm House
Pearl 6101
The Progress
Reed & Grenough

The Snug
Spruce
Tommy's Mexican Restaurant
Violet's Tavern
Whitecap
Wildseed

North Bay

Bird & the Bottle
Bouchon Bistro
Bravas Bar de Tapas
Buckeye Roadhouse
California Gold
The Charter Oak
Ciccio
Copita
Duke's Spirited Cocktails
El Barrio
Fern Bar
Geyserville Gun Club

the girl & the fig
Goose & Gander
Gran Eléctrica
Mateo's Cocina Latina
Picco
Perch + Plow
Poggio
Ramen Gaijin
Stark's Steak & Seafood
Starling Bar
Torc
Wit & Wisdom Tavern

East Bay

Bar Quiote
Bardo Lounge & Supper Club
Café Van Kleef
Comal
Commis/CDP
The Double Standard
Drexl

East Bay Spice Company
Forbidden Island
Friends & Family
Honor Kitchen & Cocktails
Hotsy Totsy Club
Juanita & Maude
Kingston 11

The Kon-Tiki
The Last Word
Mägo
Palmetto
Prizefighter
Ramen Shop
Range Life
Revel Kitchen & Bar
Sister

Sobre Mesa
Social Bird
Starline Social Club
Telefèric Barcelona
Trader Vic's
Tupper & Reed
Viridian
Walnut Creek Yacht Club

SOUTH BAY/PENINSULA

31st Union
Amandine Project
Bird Dog
The Bywater
Camper
Donato Enoteca
Ettan
Haberdasher
La Bodeguita del Medio
La Costanera
The Lexington House
LV Mar
Madera at Rosewood Sand Hill
Manresa
Mortar & Pestle Bar
Original Joe's Westlake
Paper Plane
Protégé

Puerto 27
ROOH
Saint Michael's Alley
San Agus Cocina Urbana &
    Cocktails
Telefèric Barcelona
The Village Bakery
The Village Pub

WHERE TO BUY COCKTAIL EQUIPMENT AND INGREDIENTS IN THE BAY AREA

While the Bay Area has an endless number of great bars, there are only a handful of actual stores for buying cocktail equipment. This is where the entire region comes into play as many stores and markets aren't in San Francisco.

BITTERS & BOTTLES
Between the city and the airport, this store is paradise for home bartenders and professional bartenders. They have it all—from spirits and bitters to equipment and ice molds. And, no, I'm not recommending what many of my fellow local writers mention about this shop (the proximity to SFO, flights, 3 oz. bottles).

CASK
Future Bars owns the three Cask stores. That's code for this is San Francisco's premier spirits store, plus everything you need for cocktails, except equipment and ice. Bonus: Cask has a taproom at the Berkeley store and frequent in-store tastings.

COOKIN'
Be careful walking in and ask owner Judith Kaminsky for help before being *that person* who breaks something. Literally every square inch

of this place seems to be covered with vintage cooking and bar equipment. Want retro Champagne flutes from Paris? Antique bar spoons? Bizarre goblets shaped and colored like roses that serve no function but you can figure out one for it? Yep, it's all probably here.

UMAMI MART

Located in the Temescal neighborhood of Oakland, this is a fantastic store for kitchen and bar tools imported from Japan, along with its own barware line (gold-plated shakers, anyone?). This is the place to geek out for all of your bar nerd interests. Many professional bartenders around the country order from Umami Mart online—we're lucky and can just drive there.

INGREDIENTS

Then there are the ingredients. Beyond Cask, you'll find great spirits in San Francisco at the two Bi-Rite markets, D&M on Fillmore and Gary's in Napa Valley. For fresh produce to turn into syrups and juices, well, where do I start? Farmers markets, Bi-Rite, Gus's markets, Draeger's markets, Gary's, Berkeley Bowl, Rainbow Grocery . . .the list goes on.

FURTHER READING

Of course, this isn't the only book that you should be reading about cocktails in San Francisco. Our city has dozens of highly accomplished cocktail writers who brilliantly tell the story of their own bar here in Northern California and write about subjects that are closely related to enjoying a cocktail by the Bay. I highly recommend adding these books to your library:

By the Smoke and Smell: My Search for the Rare & Sublime on the Spirits Trail by Thad Vogler

Artisanal Cocktails by Scott Beattie

Drinking the Devil's Acre by Duggan McDonnell

Batch Cocktails by Maggie Hoffman

The Joy of Mixology by Gary Regan

Jerry Thomas' Bartenders Guide: How to Mix Drinks by Jerry Thomas

Smuggler's Cove: Exotic Cocktails, Rum, and the Cult of Tiki by Martin Cate

Cocktail Boothby's American Bartender: The Anchor Distilling Edition by William T. Boothby

ACKNOWLEDGMENTS

When we started this project, nobody knew what was around the corner for the world in 2020. From the "normal" months to the dark days of the pandemic to the gradual optimism of 2021, I want to send a very heartfelt "Thank You" to the bar managers, the chefs, the restaurant owners, the bar owners, the bartenders, the distillers, the publicists, the journalists, and everyone who contributed to this book.

Thank you to Buzz and Cider Mill Press for this incredible opportunity and for your support during the pandemic.

Thank you Mom and Dad. Thank you Grandma and Gram. Thank you Collin, Beatrice, Caia, Cece, and Clutch. Thank you for being such a caring and inspiring family.

Thank you Meg and woof woof Deja. I love you both!

Thank you Jim Shelby, Eric Haskell, Mel Froli, David Tomatis, and Marcel Losier—all such incredible teachers and mentors.

Thank you Tim Farrell and Matt Struckmeyer—amazing high school English teachers who convinced me that writing actually can be enjoyable.

Thank you Erin Behan, Stephen Bassman, Anna Roth, Grant Marek, and all the editors past and present who challenge me to grow as a writer.

To the late Arthur Horowitz, who always taught me that all the world is a stage and to bring *a joie de vivre* to all the world every day.

To my late Grandpa and Granddad, thank you and we miss you. We lost Grandpa during this book process. Nobody loved the cable cars of San Francisco more than him. So many special moments with you, Grandpa. This book is for you.

ABOUT THE AUTHOR

Trevor Felch is a San Francisco-based food, drinks, and travel writer. He grew up on the Peninsula and has called the Bay Area "home" for his entire life, except for a few work or study periods in locales like Ohio, Southern California, and Paris. For a period of the 2010s, he was the Bay Area Editor for *Zagat*, covering the local eats and drinks scene during what many consider the region's modern "golden period" for noteworthy restaurants and bars openings. Today, he's one of the contributors to *Fodor's San Francisco* guide and writes a monthly wine column for the *Nob Hill Gazette*. Throughout his career, he's covered a wide variety of topics for many different publications including the *San Francisco Chronicle, SF Weekly, Palo Alto Weekly, Serious Eats, Thrillist, SF GATE, Modern Luxury Silicon Valley*, and more. He's an avid swimmer and runner, and always enjoys an afternoon at Oracle Park watching the Giants (or rooting for his other favorite team, the Boston Red Sox, from afar). When he's home by the bay or traveling, he always enjoys exploring with his girlfriend Meg and her dog, Deja.

PHOTOGRAPHY CREDITS

Pages 4-6, 28, 32-33, 51, 66, 68-69, 75, 118-119, 145, 152-153, 173, 179-181, 209, 240-243, 253, 272-273, 280, 282, 316-317, 348-349, 366-368, 372, 378, 382, 386, 388 used under official license from Shutterstock.com.

Pages 8-9, 11-13, 27 courtesy of Library of Congress.

Pages 46, 61, 227, 296, and 303 by Emma K. Morris; page 78 by Anthony Parks; page 85 by Shayana Garber; pages 98 and 101 by Ed Anderson; page 104 by Nicola Parisi; page 108 by Aubrie Pick; page 111 by Lori Eanes; page 115 by Sarah Felker; page 123 by Lauren Janney; page 151 by Marc Fiorito; pages 157-158, 260, and 262 by Edna Zhou; page 183 by Allison Webber; page 196 by Jasmin Van T Photography; page 230 by Jakob Layman; page 247 by Douglas Friedman; page 268 by Andi Miller; page 278 by Carolyn Fong; page 322 by Neil Roche; page 353 by Liz Birnbaum/The Curated Feast; page 361 by David Spiegelman.

All other images courtesy of the respective bars and restaurants.

INDEX

—ABOUT CIDER MILL PRESS BOOK PUBLISHERS—

Good ideas ripen with time. From seed to harvest, Cider Mill Press brings fine reading, information, and entertainment together between the covers of its creatively crafted books. Our Cider Mill bears fruit twice a year, publishing a new crop of titles each spring and fall.

CIDER MILL
PRESS

BOOK
PUBLISHERS
KENNEBUNKPORT, MAINE

"Where Good Books Are Ready for Press"

Visit us on the web at
cidermillpress.com

or write to us at
PO Box 454
12 Spring St.
Kennebunkport, Maine 04046